CENTRAL ASIA: SECURITY AND STRATEGIC IMPERATIVES

CENTRAL ASIA: SECURITY AND STRATEGIC IMPERATIVES

Tabasum Firdous

KALPAZ PUBLICATIONS
Delhi–110 052

CENTRAL ASIA: SECURITY AND STRATEGIC IMPERATIVES

Internation Studies

Rs. 625

ISBN: 81-7835-079-3

Published in 2002 in India by
Kalpaz Publications
C–30, Satyawati Nagar
Ashok Vihar Phase–III
Delhi–110 052
E-mail: Kalpaz@hotmail.com

Lasertypesetting at: VARSHA GRAPHICS, DELHI
Printed at: Mehra Offset Printers, New Delhi

Dedicated to my parents whom fate snatched from me before they could see it in print.

—Tabasum Firdous

Contents

Foreword

It hardly needs restating that the expansion in the direction of the Caspian Sea and the Central Asian regions was the cornerstone of the foreign policy of Czarist Russia. It continued, albeit in a different shape, after the October Revolution of 1917 when the Central Asian states federated into the Soviet Union.

The two imperial powers, Great Britain and the Czarist Russia, were bitter rivals and wanted to expand their territorial jurisdiction, the former to the north of the British Indian empire and the latter to the south in Central Asia. They made all-out efforts in either annexing the weaker states in this region or dragging them within the sphere of their strategic influence. The concept of expansion to the natural boundaries with a strong rule was the cornerstone of their policies.

The British were apprehensive of the growing influence of the Soviet Union and its prospective expansion towards the British India. They took several measures to offset this advance. One of these measures was to dispatch several missions to Turkestan with manifold aims but primarily to increase their political space in the region to check the Soviet advance. Shorn of diplomatic subterfuge, these missions were meant to convey to the Russians the political message – keep off the British Indian Empire. These were meant to fend off any possible Russian incursion into the British Indian territory.

The World War II gave a jolt to the territorial aggrandisement of super powers. But a new paradigm of "political influence" was initiated. This resulted in the creation of a bi-polar world. The Cold War phenomenon between the two super powers, i.e., the United States of America and the Soviet Union emerged. Several pacts of political and military importance like NATO, SEATO, CENTO and Warsaw Pact were signed by the countries interested in perpetuating their hegemonistic influence in the bloc of their choice. The central point of the powers was to contain the political influence of each other in the regions. The cold diplomacy flourished till late 80s, after which the Soviet system began showing signs of falling apart under its own heavy weight of subsidies coupled with the clinching state control on the economy of the Soviet Union. The Soviet diplomacy in the region lost its hold and the final blow was dealt by the Russian intervention in Afghanistan. The reformative measures to streamline the system were introduced in the form of *glasnost* and *perestroika*, which exposed the Soviet Union to the outside world and its multifarious influences. The exposure provided the Russian people a firm ground to question the viability of the socialist ideology. The process of disintegration of the Soviet system reached its climax in the last decade of the millennium. The Baltic States followed by the East European states were the first to decide for separation. Finally, the republics of Turkmenistan, Uzbekistan, Tajikistan, Kyrgyzia and Kazakhstan opted out of the Russian federation. The Trans-Caspian states followed suit. Despite the fact that the fissures in the Soviet system were emerging for quite some time, the ultimate implosion was sudden and without an option. Thus the natural consequence was full-blown chaos and confusion. Life – both literally and metaphorically – was thrown out of gear.

The arch-enemies of the Soviet Union were delighted to witness the disintegration of the system, which had posed a threat to the dominant capitalist ideology for 70 years. The traumatic situation was never visualised in a society where the state was responsible for catering to the needs of the people. The Soviet policy planners had formulated their own prescription for the development of the Central Asian region. The Soviet Union had maintained a large and well-equipped central defence system, while the republics did not have even a full-fledged police organization. The defence was in the hands of the Russians. Therefore, other nationalities were bereft of any experience in military and defence mechanism. At the same time, the very security of the republics could get jeopardized as it happened in Afghanistan where the Soviet withdrawal was followed by internecine wars and the resultant turmoil and instability. This apprehension came true in the region, especially in Tajikistan, which became the theatre for the revivalism of the Islamic ideology and the attendant role of the Saudis, Iranians and other advocates of Islamic resurgence in the region. The authorities, unnerved with the developments and without appropriate defence of the borders, were left with the only alternative of falling back upon the Russian support. The Russian forces took over the security responsibilities of frontal states, and the Tajiks practically handed down the security and defence of its southern border to the Russians. But the collapse of the Soviet system and the dismantling of the Russian military structure opened the eyes of the Slavs to a new reality hitherto unprecedented.

On the other hand, the growing influence of the USA, Europe and Japan in the exploration and exploitation of the hydro-carbon reserves of the region was an eyesore to the Russians. The diversion of the gas pipes through Caspian Sea region and Chechnya posed an open threat to the economy of Russia. It meant the deprivation of income from transit duties amounting to billions of dollars in terms of foreign exchange. The Russians, therefore, started to re-assert to halt the process of the oil transit route being snatched away. A free hand could not be given to the Europeans and the Americans in the hydrocarbon wealth of the Caspian Shelf or the Daulatabad gas field or the Tengiz oil field. In the light of nuclearisation of the Indian sub-continent, Talibanization of Afghanistan, failure of democracy in Pakistan etc., viewed in the backdrop of Central Asian developments, the security scenario of Central Asia has become critical.

In the context of this political landscape, the current study was assigned to Dr. Tabassum, a promising young social scientist. She has the relevant background of an area analyst. During the compilation of her data, she visited many centres of excellence and sought the advice of several learned scholars. I have no hesitation in affirming that she has made a sincere effort in putting down on paper in a coherent form the results of her painstaking work as also her impressions of the present state of affairs in the Central Asian Republics. The area is of crucial importance to India from all angles–social, cultural, historical, political, strategic, etc. I am sure that scholars, political analysts, policy planners and others interested in this region will read this book and derive fruitful conclusions from it.

Prof. A. M. Mattoo
Director,
Centre of Central Asian Studies,
University of Kashmir, Srinagar

October 25, 2001,

Acknowledgments

A number of my teachers, colleagues and friends have given me their full assistance in the preparation of this work. I am thankful to them. I visited many institutions and libraries to cull relevant material for the work and I thank their staff for the same.

This work was undertaken at the behest of Dr. A. M. Mattoo, Director, Centre of Central Asian Studies, University of Kashmir. Not only did he offer me very useful guidance from time to time but also agreed to write the foreword to the book for which I am beholden to him. Among my colleagues and seniors at the Centre, I am thankful to Prof. Gulshan Majid, Dr. M.A. Kaw, Dr. G. M. Mir, Dr. Aijaz Banday and all others who never hesitated in extending their assistance to me whenever I approached them. I am thankful to Prof. Shamsud-Din of SIS at JNU for his useful suggestions regarding the monograph. Mr. P. Stobdan of the Institute of Defence Studies, New Delhi gave me valuable guidance in regard to access to and the use of source material for my monograph. In particular, I am thankful to my teacher Dr. K. N. Pandita, for his useful comments.

Most of the material for this volume was obtained from some of the premier institutes and libraries like Sapru House, Jawaharlal Nehru University Library, Institute of Defence Studies and Analyses, American Centre, ICSSR, ICHR, Russian Embassy Library and many others in New Delhi. I thank them very sincerely.

My husband, Majid Jehangir gave me great moral support in my academic pursuits and I am thankful to him.

Finally, I am thankful to Dr. Pankaj Bhan of Delhi University for editing the final script and making valuable suggestions for upgrading it. My thanks are also due to the printers and publishers for bringing out the volume with great care.

Tabasum Firdous

Introduction

The collapse of the Soviet Union in 1991 was a landmark in contemporary world history and had a profound impact on the future course of human history. What is, however, surprising is that the implosion of the Soviet State was not caused by external forces, which has been the usual phenomenon behind the disintegration of established states. Undoubtedly, some external factors related to the Cold War syndrome must have been there to act as catalysts behind the collapse. But unless weaknesses and debilities inherent in the Soviet system had become so alarmingly unbearable, the collapse would not have come about. Future scholars will, eventually, address, anatomise and explain these intrinsic demerits of the system. At the moment, the debate on whether the failure is to be attributed to the intransigent leadership or to the rickety fundamentals of the socialist socio-economic ideology is on and no final picture has yet emerged.

The story of the integration of Central Asian lands into the imperial Russian State during the later half of the 19th century and thereafter by the Soviet State is not well known to the world outside. What marked Central Asia as a region having a distinct identity was its past history, its civilizational profile, its oriental life style, its landlocked topography and finally its contribution to Islam as the new religion of the East. There was nothing that could be called commonality of pattern between the westernised Russian people and orient-steeped Central Asian people. If one goes by the axiom that "East is East and West is West and the twain shall never meet" then one has every reason to believe that what the Soviet State forged was an unwilling alliance with Central Asia. And one should not forget that the Soviet State emerged as one of the two superpowers after World War II.

The collapse of the Soviet Union came as a surprise and a shock - more to the Central Asians of Irano-Aryan and Turko-Mongoloid ethnic origins than to the people of Slavic line. That should not be surprising. This phenomenon has to be understood in the backdrop of several factors. These, for example, are the transformation of the Central Asian societies from medievalism to modernism, transition of muscle energy to mechanised energy, lingering memories of despotic Khanate regimes, liberation of the vast women population from shackles of closed society syndromes, role of technological advancement in the transformation of agrarian and economic cultures, etc. For Central Asia, the Soviet system was a palpable transformation notwithstanding the means and methods that brought it about. To be precise, the history of Soviet power in Central Asia attached less importance to political structuring and ideological formulations and more importance to the net outcome in concrete economic and social terms. The outcome appeared impressive, and hence Central Asia became complacent about the political structures and the attendant ideology.

The collapse of the Soviet Union meant a sudden and dramatic end to all that was connected with the objective achievements in terms of economic development. The Central Asians had never imagined the dangers accompanying the command system and controlled economy. The first casualty in their opinion, and rightly so, was the economy of Central Asia. This was now the core issue before the Central Asians. The period that immediately followed the declaration of independence by the Central Asian republics was of intense quest for sustaining economies which rested on very fragile bases. Sections of Sovietologists are of opinion that towards the final years of the Soviet implosion, it was being increasingly realised in authoritative circles in Moscow that the Soviet State would not be able to bear the enormous burden of subsidising and maintaining the economic fabric of Central Asian states. The experts were engrossed in finding alternatives to existing economic order. However, before the new order could either be forged or set in motion, the implosion overtook the events and the rest of it is history.

With the economic ogre looking straight into the eyes of the Central Asian republics, the existing administrative machinery tried to gear itself to the new situation as quickly as was possible. It would be recalled that as the fate of the Soviet State hung in balance and the Baltic States, besides Ukraine and Bylarus, mounted tremendous pressure for secession, Central Asian republics maintained discreet silence and immobility. At that point of time, it looked paradoxical that while the Slavic people had geared up for secession, the Central Asians, so different in most walks of life and its manifestations, were complacent. This phenomenon can be explained in economic terms alone.

Economic strength and stability varied from one Central Asian republic to another. In none of the republics, natural resources had been explored and exploited to the extent to make them self-sufficient or near self-sufficient. This was because the Soviet structure needed time, resources, expertise and space to embark on an ambitious plan to cover the vast landmass called Central Asia. No doubt, some of the projects, gigantic by any standard, had been taken in hand like the Rogan hydroelectric project in Tajikistan, the space centre of Baikonur in Kazakhstan and the ambitious waterway across southern regions. Yet this was part of the long-term development plan and would have been accomplished in another century.

Hard-pressed by economic constraints, the Central Asian states found it unavoidable to join the Commonwealth of Independent States (CIS) which, in their estimation, could emerge as some guarantee against the total downslide of their economies. In doing so, they expected to be relieved of the exigency of building defence paraphernalia and security strategies, at least for some time. Under this pressure, the leaders of the Central Asian states entered into a sort of informal and unwritten agreement to avoid getting entangled in divisive issues like border demarcations, ethnic identities, communication controls, demographic complexions and complexities, etc. The underlying idea was to seek a breathing space. The statesmanship demonstrated by the leaders of Central Asian states deserves to be appreciated. The truth is that western analysts and political pundits with much limited knowledge or training of leadership under Soviet system had predicted a massive conflagration among the Central Asian states once the iron hand of Moscow disappeared. These messengers of doom were left to eat the humble pie.

In this political and social landscape, when each dollar and each pound meant a lot for the Central Asians, they joined hands to evolve a common strategy of security and defence in the eventuality of a threat emerging from any side. The gradual crystallisation of these strategies has been studied in this monograph. Soon after the formation of the CIS and streamlining of defence strategies, the situation on Tajikistan-

Afghanistan border became tense and explosive. Communism and Soviet system and not Central Asia had been the target of capitalist onslaughts during the Cold War era. As such, there was little premonition of the nature and scope of armed threat, which appeared on Tajikistan's southern border. How was this situation to be handled? If allowed to slip out of hand, its ramifications could be alarming, even tragic. All these matters brought the Central Asian leadership to an objective assessment of ground realities, possibilities and impossibilities. These matters have also been taken up for explanation and interpretation in the present monograph, and need not be repeated here.

Now as a natural sequel to the collapse of the Soviet State, Central Asia is exposed to the outside world. To some of the countries near and far, Central Asia is the new Eldorado. Various interests, ranging from economics to politics to religious identity, from ethno-cultural adventures to the romance of playing the sympathetic brother are at work in Central Asia. But lack of sufficient knowledge of the Soviet system and its achievements in terms of socio-economic infrastructures provided to the region were the main reasons for the failure of some of the adventuring neighbours in their pursuits in Central Asia. To their consternation, they soon found that there was a far stronger infrastructural base in Central Asian states than in their own countries which they considered better poised for development. New realities dawned upon them. These neighbouring states had come with various prescriptions but these fell by the wayside one by one. And when the Central Asians asked for concrete economic assistance as a test of the much touted fraternal sentiments, the euphoria vanished in thin air.

The Central Asian states, excluding Turkmenistan, are now bound by defence and security arrangement under the aegis of the CIS. Moscow obviously plays a dominating role because of her position as a military power. The only threat that is visible from outside the Central Asian fold today is from the Tajik-Afghan border. Even this is expected to be resolved through diplomatic efforts, particularly when the regime in Dushanbe has accommodated the opposition to a reasonable extent. In the present scenario, any major military threat to the security of Central Asian states is not envisioned. China has more economic interests in the region and would not like to get embroiled in petty quarrels and skirmishes. Inter-state rivalries and interests apart, no big military conflagration on that count is predicted by the analysts. These matters too have received adequate attention in the present research document.

Of all the Central Asian States, the case of Kazakhstan is noteworthy in terms of defence and security strategies. It is so because Kazakhstan has had nuclear warheads on its soil planted during the Soviet days. Thus Kazak President Nursultan Nazarbayev was right in asserting that Kazakhstan deserved nuclear power status. In the light of the nuclear disarmament policy of the US, it became imperative for Washington to denuclearise Kazakhstan. This became a tortuous process with Kazakh President wanting to extract a heavy price for a settlement. This story has been fully accounted for in the monograph. Finally, over 2,500 nuclear warheads in Kazakhstan have been, so to say, purchased off and removed from their base. But Ukraine continues to enjoy nuclear capability. That, however, does not fall within the purview of this survey.

Then remains the question of nuclear fuel available in some of the Central Asian states which could flare up tension at one time or the other. For example,

Tajikistan has deposits of enriched uranium in Khojend. Americans were apprehensive that some 'recalcitrant' states would purchase this precious matter from the Central Asian states and make use of it in producing nuclear bombs. In particular Washington subtly raised the finger towards Iran and Pakistan. Closely connected with the security concerns of Central Asia is the fact that Moscow has enjoined upon itself the obligation of ensuring non-proliferation of nuclear substance from Central Asia. How far will Moscow honour its commitment or how far will she have the power and influence to keep the commitment in place is a moot point. This has also been taken up in the monograph.

In terms of geopolitical strategies acting and interacting in the region, three powers have acquired leading roles in this region. These are the US, Russia and China. Both Russia and China are contiguous to Central Asian region. While a trans-Central Asian railway links the region with Moscow, Chinese province of Sinkiang is also linked by railway to the Kazakh lands. Central Asia also remains linked to the Persian Gulf through a railway line that runs from Ashakabad to Sarakhs and then to Bander Abbas, the Iranian sea port in the Gulf.

It is not right to call Central Asia a totally landlocked region in the background of these railroad links. Brisk trade is going on along these routes and this reminds one of the famous ancient Silk Route. As such, the geopolitical strategies adopted by external powers will have their impact on the region, its economy, security, defence requirements and the entire gamut of civil life.

Economic interests remain the supreme interest of all the three powers mentioned above. This interest has been exacerbated by the discovery of rich mineral resources, especially the hydrocarbon energy resources in Central Asia. Eventually, economic gains from these resources, when properly exploited, will spill over to the local states and some other states that have some stakes in the new developments.

In this connection the discovery of the vast oil and gas fields in Kazakhstan, enormous Daulatabad gasfields in Turkmenistan and the vast Azeri oil fields in Azerbaijan, the trans-Caspian state, are developing into major economic interests for the developed west and the US. In view of this, all the three crucial countries will try to strengthen peace in the region as peace is the first condition for economic development. Big American oil multinationals are already negotiating and have even negotiated deals with local regimes for exploration and exploitation of the energy resources in Central Asia. UNOCAL has grabbed the Azeri oil exploration and exploitation project. Iran is already having such relations with Ashakabad. Russia is keenly interested in securing her royalty interests once oil and gas pipelines begin to flow out the product through pipelines laid on Russian soil. As far as China is concerned, her experts are also present in Central Asian republics to negotiate deals.

The commonality of economic interests in Central Asia could be a good guarantee for peace and progress in the entire Central Asian region. As such, the bilateral and mutual security pacts and understanding that has been developed enjoy singular importance and credibility. It will be in no country's interests to violate these treaty regimes. As a result, one can say that an era of peace can dawn upon Central Asia and remain stable for a considerable time.

However, apart from this, one has to take into account a new phenomenon that has developed in the

Indian subcontinent, a region contiguous and close to Central Asia. This is the nuclear capability of the two subcontinent states - India and Pakistan. Though in Lahore Declaration the two countries pledged to impose full restrictions on the proliferation of nuclear arms, and agreed to observe many conditions that strongly negate the nuclear option in case of a clash between the two, yet things are very fragile in that region. A nuclear holocaust on the Indian subcontinent can have far-reaching impact on the situation in Central Asia. It could mean new alignments among forces. It could also mean interference by big powers, including China, in restraining both the countries from producing mass destruction weapons. The States like Kazakhstan have every right to ask why she is asked to denuclearise her military power while India and Pakistan so close to her have turned nuclear states. And how will things shape once Iran also enters the nuclear club?

That the Central Asian states are increasingly interested in diversification of weaponry, training, logistics and command systems of their respective forces can be gauged from the eagerness they are showing in their participation in various exercises and training courses organized by NATO under the aegis of the US. In the present study, an attempt has been made to throw some light on this aspect as well. It is very likely that in near future, many army units in Uzbekistan, Kazakhstan and Kyrgyzstan might be reorganized on American pattern and provided with arms of American manufacture.

In the matter of combating internal subversion like guerrilla warfare, anti-government insurgency, private militias, trans-border infiltration and skirmishes, narcotic mafia and the use of force etc., the Central Asian states do not have adequately trained and equipped forces to cope with any exigency. Though these challenges have not yet been posed in any of the Central Asian State on a large scale, except in Tajikistan, yet the possibility of the contagion spreading to these states cannot be totally ruled out. It has also to be understood that no doubt there are many flash points in Central Asia where ethnic strife can flare up and take a serious turn. We have seen such ugly things happening in Ferghana valley. The ethnic tensions will be a serious threat to peace and security in the region. And if these ethnic tensions are made more complicated by the religious fervour of certain groups, then, of course, the losses in terms of men and material could be substantial.

It appears that gradually the concept of CIS security may become less dependable and less significant. If peace and stability hold as of today, the Central Asian states would be fortunate enough to utilise their rare resources towards economic development and towards raising the standard of living of their people. Continued political and economic instability of Russia should caution the Central Asian states to the dangers of mutual dissension and mistrust. Nevertheless, it is interesting to watch the course of events in this most crucial part of the newly liberated region in Asia. It is no wonder that Central Asia might emerge as a stabilizing factor in the region and thus give a new turn to the course of history.

Finally, it is hoped that further inquiry in the field will be facilitated by this study. I am aware that certain discrepancies and shortcomings may have crept in here and there in this essay and I beg forgiveness of the readers for these. Research and academic pursuit is an on-going process and I hope this monograph will be a small though useful addition to that.

Tabasum Firdous

CHAPTER I

Soviet Union Hurtling Towards the Collapse

Central Asia and *Perestroika*

The huge acclaim that Gorbachev's policies of *glasnost* and *perestroika* received in the Western Soviet republics and in Europe was never duplicated in Central Asia. Every minor ethnic explosion appeared to set the stage for a larger explosion as all five communist parties refused to allow their populations to express themselves freely. They feared ethnic strife, economic strikes and an Islamic revival amongst their own people. Moreover, they feared Moscow's reaction if the Russian populations in their republics were harmed in any way.[1] They relied on the well-tried tactics of fear, repression and patronage to maintain themselves in power. Informal groups that tried to pressurise the regimes for a change or to emulate the free speech and environmental movements in Russia were banned. *Perestroika* never effectively came to Central Asia except in the shape of small, semi-underground intellectual groups. The exceptions were Kazakhstan where a strong anti-nuclear movement developed, and Kyrgyzstan where the communists ran out of ideas and promoted Askar Akaev, a non-communist professor, to become president in October 1990.

Gorbachev's accession to power in March 1985 coincided with the end of the long-running tenures of the first secretaries of the five Central Asian communist parties. By the end of 1986, all five had either died or had been ousted.[2] These men had dominated Central Asia for nearly twenty years through what was later called 'the era of stagnation'. They had built up a formidable party machine fuelled by patronage, corruption and clan loyalties. Gorbachev now had the opportunity to introduce his new policies of *glasnost* and *perestroika* through a more enlightened leadership in Central Asia which would be more sensitive to local conditions.

But what Gorbachev actually did was to replace these worthies by Russian rather than by local leaders. This was bound to create resentment at a time when national sensibilities were on the rise. He showed remarkable insensitivity to Central Asia and continued to treat the republics as colonies, which led to a rising crescendo of public resentment.[3] The first unrest in Central Asia in the period of *glasnost* and *perestroika* took place in a singularly placid area, namely Alma Ata, in Kazakhstan. In December 1986, Gorbachev removed Kazakh communist party chief, Dinmukhamad Kunayev, who had ruled the republic since 1964. He was replaced by an ethnic Chuvash from Russia, Gennady Kolbin. On 17 December, a few days after Kolbin took over, anti-Russian riots against Kolbin's appointment broke out in Alma Ata. No doubt that the riots might have been partly engineered by Kunayev's supporters, but they fed on strong Kazakh nationalist feelings in the streets.[4] At least seventeen people were killed and hundreds were injured as the riots spread to twelve other towns. Martial law had to be declared in many areas to curb the spreading unrest. The riots received immense publicity in the USSR and foreign press and shocked the ruling elite as Gorbachev was just beginning to introduce reforms in Moscow.

On the positive side, *glasnost* and *perestroika* laid the foundation for the rise of nationalism in Central Asia as also in the European Baltic republics. In the case of Central Asia, along with nationalism, Islamic dimension also surfaced in mild degrees except in Tajikistan where the drift was swift and dangerous. Nationalism had its diverse aspects depending on various elements within the given Central Asian republics. For example, in the case of Kazakhstan, initial nationalist sentiments focused on ecological catastrophes which 70 years of Soviet rule had inflicted on Central Asia. A group called Nevada-Semipalatinsk, under the leadership of the writer Olzhas Suleimanov, published literature highlighting the ecological damage caused by the 500 nuclear tests on Kazakh territory and called for an end to all further tests.[5] In Uzbekistan, a group called Birlik first emerged to protest against the drying up of the Aral Sea and the excessive development of cotton production. These groups were soon joined by a host of others, such as Rastakhez in Tajikistan, Ashar and Asaba in Kyrgyzstan and Agzybirlik in Turkmenistan. Their protests ranged from the promotion of national languages and cultures to calls for greater autonomy from Moscow and the centre. Some groups went to the extent of demanding the right to secede.[6]

With remarkable dexterity, the Central Asian leaders – with their orthodox communist backgrounds– swiftly manipulated the new nationalist currents let loose by *glasnost* and *perestroika* to their own political advantage. Gorbachev permitted his new appointees to institute more liberal social policies, to permit greater freedom of religious expression and to allow more open displays of nationalist self-expression. He only insisted that they remain loyal to the preservation of the union. With this new freedom, the Central Asian leaders quickly implemented many of the demands of the nationalist groups. During 1998-90, laws were passed to raise the languages of the titular nationalists to the status of state languages and to ensure their greater use in public life. In the same period declarations of sovereignty were announced and, following Gorbachev's example, the Central Asian party leaders transformed themselves into presidents although they remained loyal to the preservation of the Union. Karimov and Nazarbayev also went to great lengths to promote the interests of Central Asia and to show their constituencies that they were bargaining hard with the Central authorities in Moscow.[7]

Economic Legacy

The Soviet economic system in Central Asia followed classic imperialist logic.[8] The Central Asian economy was an integral part of the overall Soviet command system, primarily supplying raw materials for processing in the industrial centres of the European and western Siberian part of the Soviet Union. A large proportion of Kazakhstan's economy was devoted to the extraction of various ferrous and non-ferrous metals. Similarly, a large part of the economy of Central Asia was dedicated to the supply of cotton fiber. The Soviet economic system was also notably inefficient and wasteful of resources. This was not just reflected in the poor quality of the goods produced and their uncompetitive high costs by world market standards, but tragically, it was also seen in the ecological degradation of the former Soviet Union.[9]

Of the fine Central Asian republics in 1990, Kyrgyzstan had the lowest dependency on intraregional trade with a share of 85.07 per cent of total foreign trade, while Turkmenistan had the highest, with a share of 92.5 per cent of total foreign trade.[10] In spite of such extreme degrees of interdependence with respect to the mere functioning of the individual republican economies, the entire structure of inter-republican relations fell apart almost as soon as the Soviet Union had disintegrated. Originally, the CIS had been designed as a replacement for the Soviet Union so that cooperation between the republics, particularly in the military and economic spheres, could be maintained. It has become increasingly clear, however, that the CIS may not be anywhere nearer to this objective. Although some states like Kazakhstan are eager to make the CIS work, others, like Turkmenistan, have shown little interest in it. In an press interview, Niyazov pointedly declared :

> "There is talk about some sort of coordinating executive body within the Commonwealth's framework. We are against such a decision. I think that such a step would also resuscitate the former ... principle of managing the economy, and thus we would again be allotted the role of a raw-materials base."[11]

Central Asian Achievements under *Perestroika*

During the period of building and improvement of socialism, Soviet Central Asia attained a considerable level of social and economic development. The region made a leap forward. Efforts were made to put an end to the unequal relations between the metropolitan state and the backward outlying regions of Central Asia.

A new qualitative stage began in the inter-ethnic relations. The national oppression was liquidated and some political and economic prerequisites for gradual levelling of social and economic development of all people inhabiting the country were created. Agriculture grew vigorously on the basis of collectivization and wide development of the state property system. The most powerful irrigation complexes were constructed in this region in the recent past. Consequently, millions of hectares of desert and semi-desert land in Central Asia became the basins of highly developed cotton-growing, horticulture, viticulture, citrus gardening and stock breeding. A direct manifestation of these advantages may be seen in the transformation of the country from being a cotton-importing to a cotton-exporting one.[12] Central Asia was notorious as "the land of classical lack of roads". But the cities and villages of the whole of Central Asia were linked together with modern roads.

The most impressive achievement of Soviet Central Asia, however, is in the development of a human personality. Long before the Second World War, illiteracy was completely abolished. The problem of employment was also resolved to a certain degree. Social guarantees like social insurance, social security, free technical, general and specialized education, free medical and cultural care, etc. were provided which certainly transformed the quality of life in Central Asia.

Dimensions

After the April 1985 Plenum of the CPSU Central Committee, large-scale measures were undertaken to accelerate socio-economic development in Central Asia. These measures may be divided into two groups: measures to remedy deformations of the stagnation period, and measures aimed at gradual transition to a genuine Marxist-Leninist model of socialism taking into account internal and external features of modern development and regional specification.

First of all, the work on restoration of principles of social justice started in the region. An important move in this direction was the exposure of "cotton case". The question was not only of eradication of the phenomenon of unlawful manipulation of figures concerning the production of raw cotton, but also about the arbitrariness of cotton factories and local party and economic bodies. Cotton production and processing were integrated. Cotton factories could not lower arbitrarily actual volumes and quality of the raw cotton given by collective and state farms. The latter received full cost of the products sold to the processing enterprises. Re-establishing the principle of social justice in distribution was promoted by switching over of national economy to contract forms of labour organization and payments and to lease and rent system, especially in the field of agriculture.

In the Central Asian republics as well as all over the country, unjustified privileges were being severely criticized. The socalled "nomenclature cadres" enjoyed these privileges. The cottages, recreation zones, boarding houses, sanatoriums, hospitals and polyclinics, which had been hidden from the public, were now being transferred to general use. Special hotels created for the benefit of authorities were closed down in all towns and administrative regions. The number of special shops and their goods for government and party workers were sharply reduced.[13]

Significantly, drastic changes took place in selecting and organizing leading cadres. This was undertaken largely in the Uzbek and the Turkmen SSRs. In these republics, the staff of leading party cadres was completely overhauled at the district, regional and republican levels. Reserves of leading bodies were fully renewed, as the former ones were composed of discredited workers selected on the basis of criteria alien to socialist society. Two positive shifts were fairly promising. One was to promote capable people who had a critical attitude to all negative manifestations of the stagnation period. They could now become leading workers owing to democratisation of the whole system of selecting and organising cadres. The other was that the leaders of party and state bodies and scientific establishments began to be elected on a competitive basis with a preliminary discussion of programmes proposed by the candidates.

However, contrary to the experience of the other regions of the Soviet Union, national relations improved considerably in Tajikistan. Gradually, tension in public relations was lifted by a variety of measures. Tajiks living in Uzbekistan were oppressed under Rashidov. But after his exit, in Samarkand and Bokhara, where Tajiks constitute the overwhelming majority of the population, comprehensive schools with the Tajik language were set up, and the Tajik groups were included in the higher educational establishments. Many district and regional papers were published in two languages–Uzbek and Tajik. Leaders of high party and state bodies of Uzbekistan were ordered to eliminate the evil practice of forced assumption of a different nationality (written down in their passports Uzbek instead of Tajik). Mutual visits of republican leaders played a positive role in improving national relations in the Central Asian regions. All the members of Bureau of the Central Committee of Uzbekistan headed by the first secretary, R.N. Nishanov, visited Tajikistan and Turkmenia. They met workers, collective farmers, artists, and creative workers of these republics. Party and state leaders headed by the first secretary of the Tajikistan, namely Mahkamov, visited the Uzbek SSR. During their meetings, most urgent and up-to-date problems pertaining to relations between the republics and the two nationalities were discussed. A joint commission on national relations, with the first secretaries of these republics at the head, was set up.

The process of political *perestrokia* in Central Asia was not much different from what was happening in other parts of the erstwhile Soviet Union. Priority was given to eliminating the duplication of state and economic functions by party organizations. The transition to a new organizational structure of the party was completed everywhere. First of all, attention was paid to the reduction of the number of party functionaries. In the central committees of the Communist Party of the Union Republics, the number of departments was drastically cut, and the number of party workers was reduced by 30 per cent. Numerous branches or departments, such as water system, heavy industry, light industry, agro-industrial complex, construction, transport, etc. were eliminated. This also gave a serious blow to the directive style of management to the benefit of the administrative command system of management. Party organs restructured the area of political and ideological work as also the political guidance of social life. The thrust was on widening the democratization of social life, ensuring genuine *glasnost* and fuller realisation of the socio-economic rights of the people. Gradually, the focus of party organization's activity was shifting towards a complex of problems concerning human beings.

Yet another dimension of the problems was that during the stagnation period many people joined the party who lacked convictions, who were narrow-minded careerists and even dishonest. This was the state of party affairs in Uzbekistan and Turkmenia. However, the purge of the party ranks would not be expedient at present. Political *perestroika* also reached up to relations between union republics and central bodies of the country. The problems of perfecting these relations were tackled in the second stage of the political reform. It was discussed in detail at the Presidium of the USSR Supreme Soviet session on November 26, 1988. It is clear now that there existed the problem of harmonizing relations between the Centre and the Union Republics. Mikhail Gorbachev, in his speech at the Supreme Soviet Presidium, argued that "there should be a more clear-cut mechanism in the framework of democratization and our federal state development, which would provide for a proper level of realization of rights of the Union republics, autonomous republics, autonomous regions and districts."[14]

In accordance with the decision of the July CPSU Committee Plenum (1987), the ratio between branch and territorial management essentially changed in favour of the latter. All enterprises situated in a certain territory, irrespective of their jurisdiction, had to enrich local and republican budgets. Local and the republican bodies had the right to veto dislocation of new enterprises of Union subordination if these did not correspond to regional interests, especially if these enterprises did not contribute to the settlement of social problems or aggravated the ecological situation. Local bodies got the right to develop social infrastructures. Thus, during the two years of *perestroika*, the construction of new capital-consuming enterprises was completely stopped in Central Asia.

The rights of Union Republics were essentially extended in the field of superstructure relations. New problems were being raised in the press, television and radio such as national language, the development of literature, Central Asian history, architectural appearances of towns and villages, restoration of historic monuments, re-establishment of popular festivals forgotten during the past 50-70 years, and progressive customs and traditions. In this respect, republican cultural funds, which were set up, carried out useful work.

Beginning of the End

The Soviet Union was declared defunct on December 8, 1991, when the leaders of the Slav republics of Byelarus, Russia and Ukraine met near Minsk (Byelarus). The President of Russia and Ukraine, Boris Yeltsin and Leonid Kravchuk and the Chair of the Supreme Soviet of Byelarus, Stanislav Shushkevich, issued the following statement: "The USSR, as a subject of international law and a geopolitical reality, ceases to exist." [15] They announced that the new body that they had established - the Commonwealth of Independent States (Sodruzhestvo Nvezavisimikh Gosudarstv) - was open to all republics of the former Soviet Union and to any other state which shared its aims.

The meeting in Minsk (Byelarus) was described as intended to prevent the splitting apart of the Slav republics in the eventuality of the Soviet Union's disintegration. It followed the approval on December 4, 1991 by the USSR Soviet of the Union (lower house) of the Draft Union Treaty under negotiation since the failed coup in August.[16] As in November, Gorbachev warned of disaster if such a treaty (now intended to form a " Union of Sovereign States") binding the republics of the Soviet Union confirming the relationship between the centre and the republics were not signed. However, the Treaty's successful conclusion appeared increasingly unlikely after December 1, when

Ukraine's wish for independence was confirmed by a nine-tenths majority in a referendum, and its Supreme Soviet had subsequently voted on December 16, 1991 not to ratify any Union Treaty. A meeting between Yeltsin and Gorbachev on December 5, 1991 had concluded that a Treaty would be meaningless without Ukraine's participation.[17]

Gorbachev described the Minsk declaration as an "illegal and dangerous" constitutional coup. He attempted to use the union structures by calling on December 9, 1991 for a Congress of Peoples Deputies to be convened to discuss the Minsk agreement. The Kazakh President, Nursultan Nazarbayev, was also initially unenthusiastic over the exclusively Slav composition of the commonwealth, and at a meeting on December 9, between Nazarbayev, Gorbachev and Yeltsin, who was acting as the envoy of the Commonwealth, said that Gorbachev was still needed as a central force.

The leaders of Kazakhstan and the Central Asian republics (Kyrgyzstan – formerly Kirghizia, Tajikistan, Turkmenistan - formerly Turkmenia, and Uzbekistan), met in Ashkabad in Turkmenistan on December 12, 1991 to discuss their reaction to the Minsk declaration. They decided to become members of the CIS provided they were given the status of its co-founders.

The meeting followed the ratification on December 10 and December 12 of the CIS declaration by the original signatories' supreme Soviets. The Ukrainian Supreme Soviet made amendments to reinforce the republic's status as an independent state, including measures to strengthen border guarantees, to have its own armed forces and to bear responsibility for minorities within its borders. Nationalist deputies in Byelarus were also forwarding demands, including requests for a republican currency, a share of Union gold and currency, and control of armed forces on Byelarusian territory.

Union Treaty Negotiations

Allusion has been made to the Union Treaty in the preceding paragraphs. In fact, the real symptoms of impending disintegration of Soviet Union were reflected in the circumstances leading to the failure of the Union Treaty. The issue being of vital importance, one may try to reproduce what actually led to its disastrous end. Gorbachev announced on July 24, 1991 that, after 12 hours of negotiations with delegations from nine of the Soviet Union's fifteen republics, work on the draft Union Treaty had been completed.

This third draft of the Treaty, the most radical so far in devolving powers to the republics ("states"), had been sent for discussion to the USSR Supreme Soviet and the Supreme Soviets of the Republics at the end of June 1991. It stated that matters of defence, foreign policy, energy, communication, transport and the union budget would be decided jointly between the centre and the republics but in all other matters republican laws would have priority over union laws. Armenian Republic President, Levon Ter-Petrosyan, raised the possibility of Armenia's signing the Union Treaty. According to the Treaty, non-signatories would have to pay hard currency for their imports from the new Soviet Union.

Foreign trade officials from all 15 union republics met on July 26, 1991 and signed an agreement to divide among the republics Soviet diamond, gold and hard currency reserve, and foreign credits to the Soviet Union, as well as sharing responsibility for the Soviet Union's $ 65,000 million foreign debt. The shares would be proportional to population and gross national product.[18]

The five Central Asian republics - Kazakhstan, Uzbekistan, Kirghizia, Tajikistan and Turkmenia – reached a further agreement on August 14 to set up direct trading links between them and to reduce their dependence on central economic planning. Kirghizia had signed an economic agreement with Turkmenia on July 16, 1991 and a treaty with the RSFSR on July 21, granting Russian credit to Kirghizia and expanded economic cooperation between the republics. The president of the RSFSR and Lithuania signed a 10-year cooperation treaty in Moscow on July 29, 1991. The first clause of indefinite duration stated their mutual recognition of sovereignty. Agreements were also signed on Kaliningrad (administratively part of Russia but separated from it).

With uncertainty overshadowing the Treaty, the importance of the Union Treaty was emphasized by Gorbachev's invitation to the Presidents of the RSFSR and Kazakhstan to attend some of the summit meetings in Moscow on July 31 with US President George Bush. Yeltsin, however, refused to attend negotiation sessions jointly with Gorbachev.

Abolition of Union Structures

On December 19, 1991, Yeltsin issued three decrees bringing under Russian Federation control of all the ministries of the former USSR on Russian territory, except for the Ministry of Defence and Ministry of Atomic Power and Industry. The USSR Ministry of External Relations, established in November from the old Foreign Ministry, was abolished and its property transferred to the Russian Foreign Ministry. Embassies abroad thus came under Russian rather that

Soviet jurisdiction. The Russian Ministry of Security and Internal Affairs was established, comprising the former USSR's Ministry of Internal Affairs, the Russian Federal Security Agency and those bodies which, as approved by the USSR Soviet of the Republics on December 3, had replaced the Committee for State Security (KGB), abolished in October, the Inter-Republican Security Service and the Foreign Intelligence Service. Viktor Barannikov, the USSR Interior Minister, was appointed its head.

The administration transferred to its budget the personnel and funds (including hard currency) of the Kremlin, the USSR President's Administration and the Interstate Economic Committee (IEC) which was set up in November. The head of the IEC, Iyan Silayev, was sent to Brussels, as Russian's have control of their own resources, except gold, diamond and hard currency.[19] The USSR would drop the word "socialist" from its title to become the "Union of Soviet Sovereign Republics". Its Presidents would be directly elected, for election he or she would have to receive at least 50 per cent of total votes cast nationally and, moreover, receive this percentage in a majority to serve more than two consecutive five-year terms. There would still be bicameral Supreme Soviet. Within this, the Soviet of the Union (elected by the whole population from constituencies of equal population size) would be subordinate to the Soviet of the Republics: the latter would be elected from the Republican parliaments retaining the same number of seats as in the current soviet of Nationalists but with a single block vote for each Republic. A constitutional court would judge disputes between the union and republics and between republics. Gorbachev's hopes of signing the Union Treaty in time to present it in the mid-July 1991 G-7 Summit agreement on the future shape of the USSR were frustrated by the actions of Ukraine. Ukraine did not commit itself in clear terms to the terms of reference for the agreement.

Union Treaty Falls Through

The Ukrainian government voted on June 27, 1991 by 402 to 345 votes to postpone debating the Treaty until September 15, in order to examine possible contradictions. With Ukraine's declaration of independence of July 1990 Deputies called for Ukraine's constitution to be decided before uniting with other republics. As the Supreme Soviet debated the issue, 2000 protestors protesting against Ukraine's signing the Union Treaty were attacked outside the parliament building by Militia and by the Soviet Interior Ministry 'Black Beret" or OMAN troops with batons and tear gas.

In further negotiations with the centre on July 3, 1991, the republics' delegations demanded more concessions, including republican control over local defence industry enterprises, import-export licensing, joint control of customs and the guarantee that autonomous republics would not be allowed to sign the Union Treaty independently – an important clause for the Russian Federation, which included 16 autonomous republics.[20]

The draft Union Treaty was debated in the USSR Supreme Soviet and approved on July 12 by 307 to 11 votes with 18 abstentions, after having been approved by eight of the nine republican parliaments but not by that of Ukraine. The Supreme Soviet recommended changes to the draft treaty, which would allow direct elections to the soviet of the republics and federal taxes to be levied by the centre.

The issue of taxation was the major block in reaching agreement. The RSFSR, Ukraine and Kazakhstan had objected to allowing the federal government to impose taxes, demanding that the union budget should be financed from taxes collected by individual republics. Kazakhstan conceded the issue of federal taxation in June, however, and on July 25 the Russian Federation agreed that a fixed percentage of taxes raised from enterprises by the RSFSR government (rather than a predetermined amount as earlier demanded) would go to the union budget.

Gorbachev stated that the Treaty remained open for signature by the six republics which had declared their independence from the USSR (Armenia, Estonia, Georgia, Latvia, Lithuania and Moldavia). The presence at the negotiations for the first time of Armenia's President, Levon Ter-Petrosyan, raised the possibility of Armenia's signing the Union Treaty. According to the Treaty, non-signatories would have to pay hard currency for their imports from the new Soviet Union. Foreign trade officials from all 15 union republics met on July 26, 1991 and signed an agreement to divide among the republics Soviet diamond, gold and hard currency reserves, and foreign credits to the Soviet Union, as well as sharing responsibility for the Soviet Union's $ 65,000 million foreign debt. The shares would be proportional to population and gross national product.[21]

The five Central Asian republics - Kazakhstan, Uzbekistan, Kirghizia, Tajikistan and Turkmenia - reached a further agreement on August 14 to set up direct trading links between them and the permanent representative to the European Communities (EC). On December 28, 1991, the Russian constitutional court demanded the suspension of the decree forming the new Russian Ministry of Security and Internal Affairs until the court could rule on its constitutionality.

On December 27, All-Union Television and Radio became the Ostankino or Russian State Television and Radio Company. Yegor Yakovlev remained as its head. Yeltsin announced at the meeting in Minsk on December 30 that the first channel of Central Television would be given over to the Commonwealth, the second would be Russian, the third would be Moscow Television and the fourth would be an educational channel.

At the December 26 meeting, the deputies also released from their duties as of Jan. 2, 1992, the staff of the USSR Supreme Court, the judges of the Supreme Court of Arbitration, and the USSR Procurators' Office. Five hundred deputies called for a session of the Congress of People's Deputies to formalise the dissolution of the Soviet Union, but the call was not heeded. On December 23, the USSR Committee for the Supervision of the Constitution had dissolved itself.

The eight heads of government of the republics forming the economic community, formed on October 18, had postponed indefinitely their meeting because of "the uncertainty of the political situation". The meeting had been due to clarify agreements in the Economic Community, prior to ratification by the constituent republics' Supreme Soviet. Viktor Gerashchenko, chair of Gosbank (the USSR State Bank) resigned on December 26, 1991.

Gorbachev's Resignation

After days of speculation about his future following the collapse of any central authority in the former Soviet Union, and following a decision at the December 21, 1991 Alma Ata meeting to abolish the post of President, Mikhail Gorbachev announced his resignation on December 25 in a speech on All-Union Television.

In this resignation speech, Gorbachev asserted that although he had been in favour of "the independence and self-determination of peoples and the sovereignty of republics", he had also believed in "preserving the union state and the country's integrity". He was therefore resigning on principle. He reviewed the changes made during his period as Soviet leader saying that "a totalitarian system which deprived the country of an opportunity to become wealthy and prosperous a long time ago has been liquidated." He also expressed his hopes for the future by admitting that "some mistakes could probably have been avoided, much have been done better, but I am sure that sooner or later our shared efforts will achieve results".

After the Alma Ata meeting, Yeltsin had said at a press conference that "we do not want to follow the tradition, which has taken shape since 1917 of burying each (former) head and leader of the state and subsequently re-burying him or regarding him as a criminal". He said that the republican leaders had discussed at the meeting financial and other support for Gorbachev "in the period after his resignation", and he and Gorbachev had a long meeting on December 23 to discuss transition arrangements.

CIS is Established

On December 21, the leaders of the republics who had met in Minsk met in Alma Ata (now Almaty) in Kazakhstan. Prior to the Alma Ata meeting, Kazakhstan's President Nazarbayev had expressed his preference for the name "Eurasian Commonwealth of Independent States" for the new body. He appeared to conceive the commonwealth as a tighter union than was envisaged by the Slav republics, and the purpose of the Alma Ata meeting was negotiating the new structure rather than formally including new members, as its original founders had appeared to suggest.

Setting up of CIS Bodies

At a meeting in Minsk on December 30, 1991, the process of setting up of coordinating bodies of the new Commonwealth was discussed. Temporary agreements were signed setting up councils of heads of state and of heads of government. The supreme body was the Council of Heads of State, which would take on the responsibility of legal succession from the dissolution of the Soviet Union. The councils would normally meet in Minsk, the Council of Heads of State at least every six and the Council of Heads of Government at least every three months and both would have a rotating chairmanship. Joint sittings were allowed, as was the creation of working bodies. While the working language would be Russian, the official language would be the language of the participating states.

There was no concrete proposal made at the meeting in Minsk on December 30 to settle the economic issues affecting the member states of the CIS. A protocol was signed, however, preserving economic ties into the first quarter of 1992 and with the aim of guaranteeing over that period deliveries of the equivalent of 70 per cent of first quarter deliveries in 1991 and Askhabad were joined by those of Moldova and the trans-Caucasian republics of Azerbaijan and Armenia. Georgia, the only other former Soviet republic and the Baltic states (which had become independent in September, 1991) sent observers, but internal power struggles (including the attempt to depose the Georgain President, Zviad Gamsakhurdia), prevented Georgia's participation. The participants in the meeting signed the December 8 protocol on the formation of the Commonwealth of Independent States

(CIS). They signed a declaration which (i) stated that the CIS was open to all former Soviet States and any other countries that shared its objectives; (ii) stated that strategic forces would remain under unified control; (iii) confirmed co-operation on a single economic space, and (iv) stated that member states of the CIS agreed to honour the international obligations of the former Soviet Union. The meeting supported Russia's request to take over the Soviet Union's seat on the UN Security Council, and Russia, Ukraine and Byelarus, already UN members, pledged to support other member states' applications for full UN membership. A joint measure on nuclear arms was also agreed upon.

References

1. B. Brown, 'The Public Role in Perestroika in Central Asia', *Central Asian Survey* Vol. 9, London, 1992.

2. For more details see J. Critchlow, *Nationalism in Uzbekistan: A Soviet Republic's Road to Sovereignty*, Westview Books USA, 1990, pp. 73 et sec.

3. Ahmad Rashid, *The Resurgence of Central Asia,* London, 1994, p. 36.

4. *Ibid.* Interview with Kazakh officials 1990-91.

5. Roland Dannreuther in 'Creating New States in Central Asia", *Adelphi Paper-288*, London, March 1994, p. 15.

6. For a fuller analysis of the different informal groups, see Shireen T. Hunter, "Nationalist Movements in Central Asia", *Current History, Vol. 89, No. 549,* October 1990; and Aleksandr Verkhovskii, *Middle Asia: The Political Spectrum*, Moscow, 1992.

7. For Karimov's criticism, see James Critchlow. "Uzbeks look askance of Gorbachev's "Union" Ideas", RFE/RL research Repot, March 1, 1991. For full information on economics of Central Asia, see Kaser and Mehrotra, "Central Asian Economics and The Economic Effects of

Soviet Dissolution", London Royal Institute of International Affairs, 1993 and six IMF reports on countries of Central Asia, May 1992 and June, 1993.

8. Ruben Manatsakanian, *Environmental Legacy of the Former Soviet Republics*, Edin. 1992, p. 41.

9. Constantine Michalopoulos and David Tarr, "Energising trade of the states of the former USSR", *Finance and Development*, March 1993, p. 23.

10. *Current Digest of the Post Soviet Press* (CDPSP), Vol. XLIV (42), 1992. p. 5.

11. H. Umarov and U. Valudov, 'Prestroika in Soviet Central Asia', in The Second Revolution. *Indian Centre for Regional Affairs*, New Delhi, 1989, pp. 111 et. seq.

12. Umarov and Vahidov, loc. cit. p. 120.

13. Address by Gorbachev to Supreme Soviet Presidium, Nov. 28, 1988, Novosti Press Moscow.

14. *Keesing's Record of World Events* (KRWE), News Digest for December 1991. London, 1991. p. 38654.

15. *Ibid.* pp. 38368-73.

16. *Ibid.* p. 38581.

17. *KRWE* op. cit. p., 37617.

18. *Ibid.* p. 333491. *KRWE, op. cit.*, p. 38349.

19. *Ibid.* pp. 38320-21.

20. *Ibid.* p. 38581.

21. *Ibid*

CHAPTER II

Central Asia on the Eve of Revolution

Mikhail Gorbachev came to power in March 1985. At this point of time, by sheer coincidence and not by any design, the long running tenure of the first secretaries of the five Central Asian communist parties came to an end. Interestingly, by the end of the year 1986, all the five secretaries had either died or had been ousted from positions of power. Jabar Rusulov of Tajikistan, who had been in his position since 1961, died of a heart attack in 1982; Turdiakun Usubaliev was forcibly retired in 1985 after being at the helm in Kyrgyzstan since 1961; Mukhamednazar Gopurov of Turkmenistan retired in 1986 after running the republic since 1969; Dinmukhamed Kunayev of Kazakhstan was replaced in December 1986; and Sharif Rashidov of Uzbekistan was removed from office in October 1983 after corruption charges were brought against him.[1] In this way, these apparatchics of the ruling communist parties in the five Central Asian states got removed from the scene at more or less the same time. These men had dominated Central Asian scene for more than twenty years. Later on, this period came to be called 'the era of stagnation'. It is now learnt that they had built a formidable party machine fuelled by patronage, corruption and clan loyalties. Their exit provided Gorbachev the opportunity to introduce his new policies of *glasnost* and *perestroika* through a more enlightened leadership in Central Asia which would be more sensitive to local conditions.

But whether by design or by the urge to bring in much needed reforms in the vast region of Central Asia, Gorbachev replaced some of the outgone secretaries by Russians rather than the local leaders.[2] At a time when national sensitivities were on the rise, he created a situation which could (and indeed did) further complicate the political scenario in Central Asia. Given this state of political affairs, public resentment could not be far away.

The first unrest occurred at a place which was beyond imagination, viz. Alma Ata in Kazakhstan. The First Secretary of Kazakh communist party Dinmukhamed was replaced by an ethnic Chuvash from Russia - Gennady Kolbin. In December 1986, when Kolbin had been in office only for a few days, anti-Russian riots broke out in Alma Ata. Even if the riots were engineered by the supporters of Kunayev, these were fuelled by strong Kazakh nationalist feelings.[3] Seventeen people were killed and hundreds injured. The incident received wide publicity in Moscow and in the foreign press. This happened when Gorbachev was about to introduce *glasnost* and *perestroika* in Central Asia.

Two years later, the issue of Nagorno Karabakh exploded into war between Armenia and Azerbaijan. Crisis began in three Baltic republics followed by trouble in Georgia. Gorbachev considered these as security issues whereas there were clear indications that CPSU had failed in resolving the ethnic question in the country and especially in Central Asia. Stalin's model had totally failed. Gorbachev had never served outside Russia and had known very little about non-Russian republics of Central Asia. He had no meaningful brief on anti-Russian resentment in some Central Asian capitals and the growing feeling of ethnic nationalism and repression by local communist governments.[4]

Central Asia continued to boil. In May 1988, there were riots in Ashkabad because of the high level of unemployment among the youth. In June 1989, dozens of people were killed and about a thousand were injured in the Ferghana valley of Uzbekistan during gun battles over land and housing between Uzbeks and Meshkhetian Turks. At this time Gorbachev, speaking to pressmen in West Germany, referred to the Ferghana incidents as "Islamic fundamentalism baring its teeth". Any well-informed person could understand that this was only a dimension of ethnic unrest in the region. And this was not anything new. In February 1990, there were riots in Dushanbe and other Tajik cities over the proposed resettlement of Armenian refugees. In June 1990, gun battles between Uzbeks and Kyrgyz over land in the southern Kyrgyz city of Osh claimed dozens of lives and nearly led to war between the two republics. This was a clear indication that the two most controversial issues in Central Asia, which would dominate the future scene, were ethnicity and land. Looking in retrospect, one may say that Gorbachev's politics of *glasnost* and *perestroika* did not receive as much acclaim in Central Asia as in the western Soviet republics of those days. Conditions were far from normal in the region. The communist parties in all five republics refused to allow their people free expression. They feared ethnic strife, economic strikes and an Islamic revival amongst their own people. Above all they feared Moscow's reaction if the Russian populations in their republics were harmed in any way.[5] Thus *perestroika* never effectively came to Central Asia except in the shape of small semi-underground intellectual groups. The exceptions were Kazakhstan where a strong anti-nuclear movement developed, and Kyrgyzstan where the communists ran out of ideas and promoted Askar Akaev, a non-communist professor, to become president in October 1990 and continues to be in power even today.

Another facet of Central Asian situation at this point of time, meaning on the eve of the formal break-up of the Soviet Union, was the role of USSR in Afghanistan. The Central Asians had benefited economically from USSR's invasion of Afghanistan. By July 1987, Gorbachev had summoned Afghan President Najibullah to Moscow and told him, "I hope you are ready in twelve months because we are leaving no matter what".[6] Protests by Afghan war veterans in Moscow and Central Asia had become an embarrassment for *glasnost*. In November1987, about 2,000 veterans of the Afghan war held a meeting in Ashkhabad and decided to erect a monument for their dead. The meeting was broken up and protests against war were brutally suppressed by the police. There was large-scale public resentment.

When Gorbachev agreed to the signing of a UN sponsored agreement between Afghanistan and Pakistan in April 1988, Central Asian leaders were angry with him. They said they had not been consulted on so sensitive an issue.[7] By the time the last Soviet soldier had left Afghanistan on 15 February 1989, the Central Asian leaders felt betrayed by Gorbachev – a factor that was to influence their negative attitude towards him when the coup attempt took place in August 1991.

As power slipped from Gorbachev's hands through 1990 and 1991, Central Asian leaders hung on desperately to the old system, refusing to introduce economic reforms, liberalise the political system or open up their states to the outside world. It was more a self-conserving process than emotional attachment to a departing era. Of course, they feared that their future was uncertain and unpredictable as far as their own positions were concerned. Many of them like Islam Karimov of Uzbekistan adopted an increasingly nationalistic rhetoric in order to silence their domestic opponents and ensure some modicum of popular support. In Moscow, however, their opinion hardly mattered and was not asked for. Out of 12 Politburo members in 1989-90, only two were non-Russian; Central Asia was represented neither in the Politburo nor the Central Committee of the CPSU. Only President Nursultan Nazarbayev had become close to President Gorbachev, and he always involved himself with Gorbachev's political moves to keep the old Soviet Union together.

The breakdown of the communist structure had showed up the dormant ethnic tensions that existed down to the smallest district and even village level.[8] The Foreign Minister, Eduard Shevardnadze, resigned on January 15, 1991 warning the world of an impending military coup in Moscow. The economic crisis worsened and a coal miners' strike in March and April paralysed Kazakhstan, where some 70,000 miners went on strike. The miners' refusal to accept orders from Supreme Soviet or to accept increased pay offers demonstrated the new militancy amongst the working class.

The growth of nationalism in Central Asia was mirrored in Russia itself, where intellectuals first began to voice the need to dump the Soviet Empire if Russia was to make some meaningful progress. Central Asia was seen not as the source of raw materials, but an economic burden which was dragging Russia into backwardness. In 1991, famous Russian writer Solzhenitsyn argued that Russia would be strong if it sheds the onerous burden of the Central Asian underbelly. He called for the break-up of the Soviet Union and rebuilding of Russian nationalism. "We don't have the strength for the peripheries either economically or morally. We don't have the strength for sustaining an empire and it is just as well. Let this burden fall from our shoulders, it is crushing us, sapping our energy and hastening our demise.[9]

Boris Yeltsin won 60 % of vote in June 1991 elections. Central Asia had reason to feel disturbed. He had far less interest in Central Asia than Gorbachev had. He would not hesitate to take Russia out of the Union if it helped his political career. If Gorbachev was considered weak and vacillating, then Yeltsin was seen as erratic, temperamental and unpredictable.[10] For the time being, in the event of growing tension between the two leaders, Central Asia got out of focus of world politics. Gorbachev tried to negotiate a new Union Treaty that would devolve powers from Moscow to the republics. On 24 July 1991, he announced that he and leaders of ten republics had agreed on a power-sharing treaty. By 20 August 1991, the treaty was ready for signing, but a day earlier the coup makers made their bid to topple Gorbachev and scuttle the new Union Treaty. A discussion on the legality of the coup is outside the scope of this study. But suffice to say that before it took place, 20 per cent of the card-holding members of he CPSU had already resigned. There was a crisis of political and economic confidence, and whereas communists saw the breaking of the Union as high treason, non-communists saw it as not progressing fast enough. Gorbachev could not satisfy either camp. The economic crisis worsened and the centre just ran out of money as the provinces refused to pay taxes.[11]

Some erroneous opinions have been built on the question of Central Asia's reaction to the coup of 1991 in Moscow. In fact, Central Asia's reaction could be called as stunning. Only the non-communist leader Askar Akaev moved troops into the Kyrgyz capital Beshkik in order to prevent a communist coup taking place. He immediately condemned the Moscow plotters. The Kazakh President, Nursultan Nazarbayev, who had stood by Gorbachev, said nothing for the first thirty-six hours as he watched which way the wind blew. Finally, two days after the coup, he condemned it but only after it became clear that the coup was failing. The leaders of Uzbekistan, Tajikistan and Turkmenistan openly supported the coup plotters and immediately used the coup to crack down on their own dissidents.[12]

The coup failed and these leaders rethought their positions. On 24 August 1991, Gorbachev banned the CPSU which led to the dissolution of communist parties in Central Asian republics. Five days later, the Supreme Soviet upheld this decision. Dushanbe reacted violently, and on 7 September opposition rallies forced the first secretary Kahhar Mahkamov to resign. He thus became the first political casualty of the end of communism in Central Asia. The Tajik republic plunged into a disastrous civil war.

Regional Groupings

Gorbachev failed to win the support of the republics for a new Union Treaty, and this deadlock prompted the three Slav republics to set up the Commonwealth of Independent States (CIS) without even consulting the Central Asian republics. Finally, the newly enlarged CIS was formed on 21 December 1991 in Alma Ata and four days later, on Christmas Day, Gorbachev resigned.

The CIS is noteworthy for the fact that in it 10 opinions, that are the 'only correct' ones, coexist. Out of the diversity of opinions one single comment by Leonid Kravchuk may be an indicator. He said, "It would be even worse if CIS didn't exist, but that not everything has to be decided within the framework of the CIS, that it doesn't have to be regarded as an all-embracing structure."[13]

The Central Asian states have been spawning political and economic associations with the purpose of shaping their regional identity. In February 1992, the newly independent Central Asian states were invited to become the members of the Economic Cooperation Organisation (ECO) founded 25 years ago by Iran, Turkey and Pakistan, then called the Regional Cooperation for Development (RCD). Except for Kazakhstan, which preferred to be an observer, the other four opted for full membership in the Islamic bloc.

In the ECO summit, the major emphasis was given to create a powerful Islamic Common Market and elimination of all tariff and non-tariff barriers, including export subsidies. It also talked about common faith, cultural affinities and shard experience of history. Akhtar Adil Rizvi, a Pakistani analyst remarked, "Cooperation of the kind envisaged in terms of need and feasibility may be limited to economic interaction for the time being. It can also blaze the trail to new perspectives. The bonds of history and cultural affinity combined with contemporary imperatives of security in a volatile political and strategic environment ought to enlarge the scope and capacity of their cooperation and collaboration."[14] Hoping that Afghanistan and Bangladesh might also be inclined to join ECO, Rizvi commented, "Ironically, it is this strength which is causing nightmares in some Western capitals, raising scenarios of the emerging coalition of states (particularly Iran, Pakistan and Kazakhstan) producing 'Islamic' nuclear bombs and becoming a citadel of extremism. After the disintegration of the Soviet communist empire, Islamic fundamentalism with all its alleged diabolical attributes is supposed to be increasingly threatening western capitalism.[15]

Admission of non-Islamic states such as Armenia in the ECO was also debated. Pakistan officials felt that Armenia's membership would be considered if it applied for membership. Alongwith Turkey, Pakistan wishes to develop the ECO as an economic entity and not as an Islamic group. But President Rafsanjani of Iran viewed the ECO as an "Islamic political-economic organization which could develop into a world power". Stretching from the Balkans to the Himalayas and covering a combined population of 250 million people, if the ECO is launched successfully, it may have wide-ranging implications. But at the moment, there are divergent interests of each country, particularly Iran and Turkey, who have their own rival regional interests in forming economic institutions. For example, Teheran has spearheaded the Caspian Sea Cooperation Zone to include Iran, Azerbaijan, Kazakhstan, Russia and Turkmenistan. Turkey, however, decided to launch the rival Black Sea Cooperation Council to include Turkey, Azerbaijan, Bulgaria, Romania, Ukraine, Georgia, Armenia, Moldova and Russia.[16]

The need to construct a qualitatively new relationship with Russia has been the most complex and sensitive post-Soviet challenge for the Central Asian States. The distinctive legacy of Russian imperial practice and its penetration into Central Asia has only magnified the sensitivity of this challenge. Unlike the French or the British Empires, the Russian and Soviet

Empire was contiguous to Central Asia. Combined with highly centralised nature of the Soviet system, the economic, political and military links between the different parts of the empire were far more embedded than French or British links with their predominantly trans-Atlantic empires. The presence of ten million ethnic Russians in Central Asia and large Turko-Muslim nations in the Russian Federation, such as the Tatars (Tartars) and Bashkirs, highlights the demographic interconnectedness of the Russian Soviet Empire. This necessarily makes the imperial separation of Russia from Central Asia a more difficult and potentially more destabilising process than other analogous imperial disengagements, such as the British withdrawal from India. The Russian government is naturally sensitive to any perceived or actual threats to Russian brethren remaining in Central Asia.[17] For their part, the Central Asian government can hint at major domestic unrest within Russia if Central Asian interests are not respected by the authorities in Moscow.

The absence of a nation building anti-colonial struggle in Central Asia adds another distinctive feature to the post-imperial Russian–Central Asian relationship. Unlike other regions of the former Soviet Union, such as the Caucasus, Ukraine or the Baltic states, the Central Asian States gained their independence without a popular anti-Russian uprising. The leaders of the newly independent states were far from being nationalist firebrands; they had, in fact, been faithful members of the Soviet Communist Party and advocates of close links with the political hierarchy in Moscow after long careers as obedient servants of the Soviet apparatus. Their instinctive response to the disintegration of the Soviet Union was to seek a new relationship with Russia, which would protect rather than destroy the old links. In part this reflected a realistic appreciation, absent from many of the more nationalistic post-Soviet governments and many critical dependencies of the Soviet system, particularly in the security and economic fields.

But this syndrome also highlighted a deep-seated fear of the consequences of losing Moscow's guiding hand — the natural reflection after a century of treating Russia as the 'elder brother' whose will defined the political, economic and social network of Central Asia. This sense of the necessary imperial subordination of Central Asia has also left its mark on the Russian consciousness. The popularity of the political programme of Vladimir Zhirinovsky in December 1993 Russian elections revealed the continuing vitality of the Russian imperial mentality.[18]

It is important, however, to be careful in suggesting a Central Asian inferiority complex towards Russia or Russia's determination to perpetuate its imperial control over Central Asia. There are also powerful pressures from both sides to consolidate the process of imperial separation. The leaders of the Central Asian states are far from willing to cede the newly acquired sovereignty of their states to the dictates of Moscow. For essentially opportunistic reasons, the Central Asian leaders have become committed independent nationalists, seeking to promote full political and economic independence of their countries. Any neo-imperialist statements emanating from the Russian governments are unambiguously condemned in the Central Asian press. There are other possibilities of alliance with neighbouring countries like China or countries in the Middle East. If Russia were to revert to its traditional imperial disposition, it is probable that the Central Asian states would adopt a far more hostile attitude.

Inter-Regional Dependence

However, this is not the only perspective of relationship between Russia and the Central Asian states. There are others which tell a different story. That the disintegration of the Soviet Union may have disrupted relative stability within individual republics, that it has completely destroyed whatever relationship existed between them - is one more opinion. Moscow's ruling elite had always sought to prevent the self-sufficiency of the individual republics. Thus, the source of industrial input and production virtually always differ.[19] None of the 14 Republics (other than Russia), and certainly none of the Central Asian Republics, enjoys any degree of agricultural diversification. Agriculture in Uzbekistan and Tajikistan consists almost exclusively of cotton cultivation. Thus, interdependence in agricultural and industrial production resulted in exceptionally high degrees of interdependence in trade as well.

Of the five Central Asian republics in 1990, Kyrgyzstan had the lowest dependency on inter-regional trade with a share of 85.7% of total foreign trade, while Turkmenistan had the highest with a share of 92.5% of total foreign trade.[20] In spite of such extreme degrees of interdependence with respect to the mere functioning of the individual republican economies, the entire structure of inter-republican relations fell apart almost as soon as the Soviet Union had disintegrated. Originally, the CIS had been designed as a replacement for the Soviet Union, so that cooperation between the republics, particularly in the military and economic spheres, could be maintained. It has become increasingly clear, however, that the CIS is not achieving this objective. Although some states, like Kazakhstan, are eager to make the CIS work, others, like Turkmenistan, have shown little interest in it. Niyazov pointedly declared in an interview to the national press.

> There is talk about some sort of coordinating executive body with the commonwealth's framework. We are against such a decision. I think such a step would also resuscitate the former... principle of managing the economy, and at this point we cannot entirely rid ourselves of it. In any case, that way we would again be allotted the role of raw-material base.[21]

President Niyazov of Turkmenistan instead expressed a preference for pursuing bilateral relations with other republics, arguing that that was the only way in which agreement between them could be reached.[22] This, however, may be easier said than done because, in addition to economic obstacles such as discrepancies in fiscal management, trade barriers, pricing policies etc., there are also significant and potentially volatile political obstacles to cooperation. Territorial disputes alone could make cooperation in any sphere a difficult, if not an impossible, task.

Potentially the most contentious dispute is between the Uzbeks and the Tajiks. Central Asia's two main Farsi speaking cities, Samarkand and Bukhara, were included in Uzbekistan, leaving the Tajiks with the backwater town of Dushanbe for their republic's capital. For their part, the Uzbeks have periodically staked a claim to all of the Ferghana valley, which includes Kyrgyzstan's Osh oblast, and part of the Khojend (formerly Leninabad) oblast in Tajikistan. The Uzbeks also argue that parts of southern Kazakhstan and eastern Turkmenistan rightfully belong to them as well. The republics of Kyrgyzstan and Tajikistan disagree not only about where their border should be, but even where it is, and briefly came to blows over this question in the summer of 1989.[23]

Regional Groupings

Surprisingly, however, just when it appeared that cooperation among the Central Asian republics was destined to fail in the short and medium terms, the leaders of the five republics announced on 4 January, 1993 the formation of a five-state Central Asian Common Market. Citing their frustration with Russia's apparent inability to create a viable institutional framework for the CIS, the heads of state have apparently decided to give regional cooperation one more try.[24]

Regardless of the outcome of this latest attempt at cooperation, it is crucial that the development strategies designed for the national scene be adjusted to take account of this regional development. Failure to do so may well destroy all chances of cooperation, particularly because of the importance of coordinated policy-making, given a common currency and high inter-republican trade dependency.

A number of regional groupings involving some or all of the new Central Asian states have already emerged. Among these are the Economic Cooperation Organization (ECO) founded by Turkey, Iran and Pakistan in the late 1980s. In November 1992, the membership was officially expanded to include Afghanistan and the former six Muslim Soviet republics. Turkey has been making overtures on behalf of the Turkish Republic of Northern Cyprus, while Rumania has also been seeking admission. The organization itself is still in its formative stages although by 1996 it was able to gain some consolidation. Iran and Turkey are definitely disagreeing on the direction it ought to take. While Turkey is seeking an economic organization modelled after the European Union, Iran is pursuing a sort of 'Islamic Commonwealth'.[25]

Such agreements, however, do not mean that ECO has no potential benefits to offer to its Central Asian members. First, ECO provides alternative trading route to Central Asian States whereby access to the Persian Gulf via Iran is particularly important. Second, coordination in the energy sector involving especially the more efficient distribution of Central Asian electricity surpluses and Iranian resources will be a fundamental first step to the improvement of much needed infra-structure. Third, with an assured market of around 250 million people, the small goods manufacturing sector stands to benefit in all member countries. Fourth, many informal economic activities of transnational proportion, such as border-area black markets and unrecorded cross-border trade, could be controlled more effectively under the auspices of ECO for the purpose of extracting revenue through taxation. Other issues, such as population migration, arms trade, drug trafficking and ecological degradation could also be dealt with effectively within an institutionalized framework of regional cooperation.

Ultimately, while regional cooperation within Central Asia and cooperation between Central Asia and its immediate environment (especially the Middle East) will not by itself solve the region's development problems, the potential benefits of a regionalist policy-orientation should become part and parcel of the individual state's development strategies.

In any case, having formed the CIS, the task remained at least for the Central Asian republics to consolidate the efforts for the realization of the purpose for which the organization had been brought about. This consolidation process, in actuality, was initiated in Bishkek Conference in 1993. This could be considered a watershed in the short history of CIS vis-à-vis Central

Asia. Members of the Bishkek conference confirmed their support for a stronger CIS. The Bishkek conference of the heads of states of Central Asia and Kazakhstan, which finished its work on 23 April, passed a final resolution.[26]

The leaders of the 'Asian Group of Seven' particularly stressed that the meeting was not held in a political isolation nor was it aimed at setting up an alliance or political grouping. Six agreements were signed by the leaders. These included the need to build a trans-Asian railway and highway linking Istanbul, Teheran, Islamabad, Ashkabad, Tashkent, Bishkek and Alma Ata.[27] It was also decided to design and build a gas pipeline for the transportation of natural gas from Turkmenistan to Iran, Turkey and the European countries. The agreement signed by the Central Asian members of CIS and other regional states in Ashkabad in May 1992 was as follows:

Agreement on economic cooperation in the implementation of "projects of mutual interest".

Guided by the principles of friendship and solidarity, Iran, Kazakhstan, Kyrgyzstan, Pakistan, Turkey, Turkmenistan and Uzbekistan hereby agree upon the following:

1. To accelerate the construction of a Trans-Asian railway. To complete the construction of the Sarakhs-Meshed section by 1995, and to speed up the development of the Druzhba (Friendship) station of the border railway section linking the Republic of Kazakhstan and the People's Republic of China.
2. To design and build a gas pipeline that would supply natural gas from Turkmenistan to the Islamic Republic of Iran, to the Turkish

Republic and to Europe in the following volumes: 15 billion cubic metres a year at the first stage and 28 billion cubic metres a year at the second stage. The states concerned shall ensure the transit of gas from Turkmenistan through their territories during at least 30 years.

3. The signatories to the agreement have found it expedient to design, build and reconstruct sections of the highway linking Istanbul, Teheran, Islamabad, Ashkabad, Tashkent, Bishkek and Alma Ata, pending the opening of international motor communication. To implement the said projects, the signatories have found it expedient to set up corresponding coordinating councils consisting of the leaders of corresponding bodies.

At the end of Ashkabad meet, the participating Central Asian leaders issued a joint communiqué. Its text ran as this:

The Presidents and Prime Ministers of Iran, Kazakhstan, Kyrgyzstan, Tajikistan, Turkmenistan and Uzbekistan state as the following:

1. Proceeding from the belief that economic and trade contracts constitute a considerable part of their relations, the parties will make efforts to broaden trade and develop joint investment projects.

2. The parties will exchange delegations, organise exhibitions and conferences, and other events facilitating the sale of goods and services.

3. The parties have expressed readiness to exchange goods mutually.

The conference members ... respecting the right of each state to independent development, recognizing and respecting the territorial integrity of the states and the inviolability of the present borders between them, undertake to:

1. Renounce the use of force or threats of using force in their relations.
2. Renounce any interference in the internal affairs of the states-members of the conference.
3. Rely on the principles of close cooperation, consultations and all round assistance in resolving economic, social and cultural and political problems.
4. Observe international treaties and pursue a joint policy of regional security, disarmament and control over weapons, participate in the drafting and implementation of programmes aimed at cutting weapons and armed forces on their territories.
5. Observe international agreements on human rights and guarantee main civil rights to their population, including the rights of ethnic minorities.
6. Recognize main principles of the democratic process and political development to call on all the political parties and public movements in their respective states to respect constitutional norms and the lawfully elected power bodies.
7. The members of the conference voice their

support for the development of equal and mutually beneficial economic, political and humanitarian cooperation with the neighbouring Asian States all the more so that the peoples of the member-republics and those Asian states enjoy deep-rooted traditional links going back to ancient times.

8. The members of the conference believe that current events in Afghanistan are an internal affair of that sovereign state and call on all the interested parties for a dialogue supporting the UN initiative on a peaceful settlement of the conflict.

9. The heads of the states-signatories to the present address emphasise the need for regular summits and intend to coordinate their activity in the areas of mutual interest in the framework of the CIS as well as at the commonwealth as a whole.

It has been already said that the president of Turkmenistan had initially some reservations about the CIS and ECO. Therefore, Turkmenistan decided not to sign some of the documents submitted at the Bishkek summit arguing that the situation in Turkmenistan was somewhat special. However, Turkmen President, Saparmurad Niyazov took the initiative in organising another meeting of the leaders of Central Asian states in Ashkabad in May 1992.

The thrust of the Ashkabad meeting was intended to be on the economic issues rather than on forming any political bloc. President Niyazov was cited as saying that "in Bishkek, they tried to impose on us the creation of some special structures. But why do we need yet another superstructure? We must not implant artificial formations that have a more political than economic significance".[28]

Two states – Kazakhstan and Kyrgyzstan – had begun as far back as 1991 the process of enacting legislation that would allow a capitalist economy, private property and foreign investment with repatriation of profits. Other republics had taken no such steps when independence dawned and they continued to vacillate about such legislation through 1992. The overall first experiences with privatisation were not good. Even states advanced in legislation for privatisation, like Kazakhstan, chose the most unprofitable state-owned companies or the farm with the poorest land to be sold off first to either workers committees or groups of individual buyers. The results were open to easy criticism by communist hardliners who continued to criticise any overhasty change to private enterprise.[29]

The question of currency was no less acute. In late 1992 the growing economic crisis convinced hardline nationalists and communists to pressurize their leaders to leave the rouble zone and set up their own independent currencies. However, president Nazarbayev and Akaev opposed this. At a CIS summit in October 1992, Nazarbayev was instrumental in persuading the CIS to rationalise the rouble zone by setting up an Inter-Union Bank to create a unified financial system. "It would be absurd for Kazakhstan or anyone else to leave the rouble zone and try and declare financial independence from Russia. This is still an inter-dependent economy. These are just the demands of sentimental nationalists who don't understand economics," said Dr. Chan Young Bang, the South Korean adviser on economic affairs to President Nazarbayev.[30]

It is pertinent to refer briefly to the financial disaster with which Central Asian republics and Russian Federation as well were confronted in the early days of CIS. Almost every section of the community suffered under the staggering economic crisis. This can be judged by the near collapse of the newspaper industry within the space of a few months because of the rising cost of paper which was imported from Russia. The leading Kyrgyz daily newspaper, *Kyrgyzstan Titsu,* established in 1924, had a print run of 185,000 copies in 1991. In the first few weeks of 1992, the cost of newsprint rose from 8.30 to 22.00 roubles a ton. The newspaper was forced to restrict printing to 80,000 copies, laid off workers and asked the government for a subsidy to help defray the cost of newsprint. Journalists maintained that after the shortage of food and petroleum, the biggest shortage in Central Asia was that of paper. In 1991, the Writers' Union of Kyrgyzstan published over 150 new books. In 1992 it could not publish a single book because of the cost of paper.

In Central Asian capitals, finance ministers looked to the West and the Far East for investment, while they glanced only half-heartedly at the Muslim countries of Iran, Pakistan, Turkey and the Gulf region which were wooing them. But by 1993 the republics had realised that little was coming from the West and they had better seriously respond to offers from the Muslim south. This led to the first comprehensive economic plan to develop communications and other economic infrastructure in the region agreed at the Foreign Minister's meeting in Quetta, Pakistan, on the advantageous party basis, to grant each other the most favoured nation status and to set up joint banks and small and medium enterprises. The parties agreed:

1. Attaching great importance to the establishment and development of motor, railways, air and sea transportation and lines of communication, the parties have agreed to develop and implement bilateral and multilateral projects in the said areas.
2. The parties note that the construction of gas and oil pipelines, the production of oil and gas and the building of refineries will allow them to ensure normal economic development of the given region and to transport natural gas and oil to other countries.
3. The parties have agreed to consider the possibility of introducing soft customs duties and a simpler procedure of crossing the border to ensure free movement of people and goods through their territories in accordance with international provisions and agreements.
4. With the purpose of promoting tourism and improving mutual under-standing in the region, the sides will jointly study each other's culture and history and restore historical and cultural monuments.
5. The parties note that the Economic Cooperation Organisation plays an important role in broadening mutual cooperation and agree that the members of this Organisation should make every effort to attain its goals.
6. The parties emphasise that by broadening regional cooperation they pursue no plans for establishing any blocs threatening the interests of other states.
7. The parties have agreed to instruct their foreign ministers to explore the possibility of

convening a conference on interaction and trust-building in Asia.

8. The parties find it expedient to hold regular consultation on problems of mutual interest.

Bilateral and Multilateral Facets

It has been noted that in the Bishkek meeting of 23 April 1992, the vastly differing approaches to the market economy and the reluctance of some states to legislate for privatization came to the surface. Turkmenistan differed on privatization, while Uzbekistan refused to consider a common pricing policy and wanted to retain large subsidies on foodstuffs because of the political fallout of the food riots. Apart from Turkmenistan, however, all the republics signed documents which increased their inter-state cooperation in banking, transportation and trade. They all now faced one common problem. Russia was no longer bankrolling their budget and they all needed to generate their own revenue through new taxation and exports. This could only be carried out by encouraging private enterprise and foreign investment[30] among members of Economic Coordination Organisation (ECO), which comprised ten countries of the region including the five Central Asian states.[31]

References

1. J. Critchlow, 'Nationalism in Uzbekistan: A Soviet's Road to Sovereignty', *Westview*, USA, 1991, p. 63.
2. Ahmad Rashid, *The Resurgency in Central Asia*, London, 1994, pp. 35-36.
3. H. Smith 'The New Russians', *Vintage*, USA, 1990. p. 121.
4. Doder and Branson, *Gorbachev: Heretic in the Kremlin*, London, 1990, p. 83.
5. *Ibid.*

6. Doder and Branson. *op. cit.* p. 69.
7. 'Central Asian Republics Must be Consulted', Ahmad Rashid, *The Nation*, Lahore, 19 December 1991. Also see *Independence*, London, 17 December 1991.
8. S. Crawshaw. *Goodbye to the USSR: The Collapse of Soviet Power*, London, 1992, p. 76.
9. A. Solzhenitsyn, *Rebuilding Russia*, London, 1992, pp. 48 et. seq.
10. Ahmad Rashid, *loc. cit.* p. 39.
11. S. Crawshaw, *op. cit.* p. 79
12. Ahmad Rashid, 'Muslims: Chance to Seek More Power', *The Independent*, London, 22 August 1991.
13. P. Stobdan, 'Central Asian Regional Security', *Strategic Analysis vol. XV No. 5*, New Delhi, Aug. 1992 pp. 472-73.
14. A. A. Rizvi, 'ECO for Regional Cohesion', *Pakistan and Gulf Economist, 22, 28* February 1991, p. 2.
15. F. Stobdan, *op. cit,* p. 473.
16. Roland Dannrcuthor, 'Creating New States in Central Asia', The International Institute of Strategic Studies, (*Adelphi Pager – 288*) London, 1994, p. 52.
17. *Adelphi paper – 288, op. cit,* p.53.
18. Kiaras Gharabaghi, 'Development Strategies for Central Asia in the 1990's: In Search of Alternatives'. *Third World Quarterly, Vol. 15, No. 1*, London, 1994, p. 113.
19. Constantine Michalopoulos & David Tarr, 'Energizing Trade of the States of the Former USSR', *Finance and Development*. London, March 1993, p. 23 (table).
20. Current Digest of the Post- Soviet press (CDPSP), XLIV, (42), London, 1992, p. 5.
21. *Ibid.*
22. Martha Olcott, 'Central Asian's Post-Empire Politics', *Orbis*, Spring, Note 13, p. 256.
23. For details, See *CDPSP, XLV (I),* 1993, pp. 1-8.
24. Kiaras Gharabaghi, *op. cit.*
25. P. Stobdan, *op, cit.*
26. P. Stobdan, *op. cit.* P. 474.

27. A. A. Rizvi, 'ECO for Regional Cohesion,' *Pakistan and Gulf Economist, 222-28* February, 1991, p. 6.
28. Ahmad Rashid, Interview, Nov-Dec. 1991, *op. cit.* p.69.
29. Ahmad Rashid, 'The Next Frontier', *Far Eastern Economic Review*, London, 4 Feb. 1993.
30. Ahmad Rashid, *The Resurgence of Central Asia*, *op. cit.* p. 69.
31. These were Iran, Pakistan, Turkey, Afghanistan, Azerbaijan, Kazakhstan, Kyrgyzstan, and Tajikistan. The Quetta Declaration of 7 February 1993 set out the new economic plan. See Ahmad Rashid, 'Linking up with Trade', *Far Eastern Economic Review*. London, 25 February 1993.

CHAPTER III

Sovereignty, Defence and Political Structure

Sovereignty

It will be seen that even at the most basic level of Central Asian identity, the period of Russian rule has left an indelible impression. Some of this is attributable to the partial success of Russian and Soviet attempts to assimilate the subject people of the empire including those of Central Asia. The Tsarist military historian, Mikhail Venyukov, emphasised this distinctive aspect of Russian imperial policy by comparing Russians to "Englishmen in India who do their utmost to avoid mingling with the natives.... Our strength lies in the fact that.... we have assimilated subject races, mingling affably with them."[1]

Although the Soviet ambition of forging a supranational imperial identity was rejected when the Soviet Union disintegrated in 1991, it left its mark on the development of Central Asia's identity. The post-Soviet Central Asian leaders have been remarkably frank about their countries' past debt and continuing dependence on Russia. President Nursultan Nazarbayev of Kazakhstan noted that his country "is tied to Russia not even by thousands, but by millions of threads and millions of human destinies".[2] The belief of President Islam Karimov of Uzbekistan that "we need Russia like the air, like water..... no less important is our spiritual kinship" reflects a common view amongst the Central Asian ruling elite.[3] These statements are in striking contrast to the deliberate rejection of such close Russian links by the Baltic, Ukrainian or Caucasian post-Soviet nationalistic leaderships.

Another factor that sheds light on the usually benign attitude towards Russia's historical role in Central Asia is that this region has had no pre-Russian heritage. It was Russian and Soviet administrators who demarcated them and then set about building nations to fit the states. The Russian and Soviet involvement in nation-building was especially strong amongst the nomadic groups, the Kazakhs and Kyrghyzs in particular, who were isolated from the modern world and had only oral, if lively, cultural traditions. With Russian help, written Kazakh and Kyrgyz languages were created, historical sagas were transformed into national myths and territory was designed as their rightful property.

Ethnicity and Statehood

Political unity has been a rare historical commodity in the history of Central Asia. The deeply entrenched divisions between sedentary and nomadic and between the Persian and the Turk have traditionally prevented the formation of clearly defined unified states. Only Tamerlane succeeded in welding together a unified Central Asian polity, but the short duration of his dynasty revealed the brittleness of this political construct. Prior to Russian annexation, Central Asian states did not attempt to forge a specific ethnic or nationalist identity and their borders were broadly determined by the contingent extension of imperial power. Therefore, it becomes a very complicated matter to talk of these republics in terms of defined states and with sovereignty

Within these loose state formations continually expanding and contracting with the military fortunes of the ruling elite of the time, the peoples of Central Asia were free to express a variety of overlapping identities. The most basic of these was related to place or lineage, to region and clan for the oasis dweller, and to tribe and tribal confederation for the inhabitants of the Steppes.[4] Another source of identity was cultural or ethnic, principally focused on association with the Turkic or Persian family of nations. The third and potentially the most unifying source of identity was Islam, which, by the late nineteenth century, had penetrated the farthest reaches of Central Asia, incorporating, at least formally, the previously Shamanist Kyrgyz and Kazakh into the *Daru'l-Islam*. What did not emerge from these multiple and overlapping sources of identity was a clearly defined national consciousness on the European model of nation-state consolidation.

The Stalinist redrawing of the borders of Central Asia became apparent with the unraveling of Soviet Empire. From 1989 to 1990, there was a series of riots in Central Asia which had clear ethnic as well as social and economic dimensions. The bloodiest of these riots occurred in June 1990 and pitted the Uzbek against the Kyrgyz in the city of Osh in the Ferghana valley resulting in over 320 deaths.[5] There were numerous other territorial or ethnic disputes which were only barely repressed: Tajik claims to the towns of Samarkand and Bukhara, conflicting Kyrgyz-Tajik claims to the Isfarah region on their border, Russian claims on the northern oblasts of Kazakhstan, and demands by Gorno-Badakhshan and Karakalpakstan for greater autonomy or even independence.[6]

Stalin's principal political objective in structuring a new ethnically based order was to prevent the diffusion of other potentially more powerful and integrative political identities. In the late nineteenth century, Central Asian intellectuals assembled under the banner of the *Jadidist* (Renewal) movement led by the Tartar Ismall Bey Gasprall (1851-1914) who had been promoting the idea of a unified Turkestan with an Islamic identity, but with a modern, progressive political and social programme. The Bolshevik revolution had undermined the liberal democratic veneer of this movement. However, the *Jadidist* spirit was inherited by some of the leading Central Asian Bolsheviks, such as the Uzbek Fayzullah Khojaev and the Kazakh Ali Khan Bukeykhanov, who tried to establish a Muslim national communism, which would defend the unity of Central Asia and free it from imperial subordination to Moscow.[7] Stalin's political objective in giving Central Asia a divided ethnic identity was to destroy the pan-Turkic and pan-Islamic nationalist currents championed by the Central Asian political elite. The liquidation of most of this elite in the purges of the 1930s marked the brutal climax of this ideological campaign.

Nationalist and Islamic Dimensions

Following the example of the Baltic States and the Caucasus, informal groups in Central Asia began to express dissent in the more liberal atmosphere of the late Gorbachev period from 1988-91. Their initial areas of concern were the ecological catastrophes, which 70 years of socialist rule had inflicted on Central Asia. In Kazakhstan, a group called Nevada-Semipalatinsk, under the leadership of the writer Olzhas Suleimanov, brought to light the ecological damage caused by the 500 nuclear tests on Kazakh territory and called for an end to all further testing.[8] In Uzbekistan, a group called Birlik first emerged to protest against the drying up of the Aral Sea and the excessive development of cotton production. These groups were soon joined by a host of others, such as Rastokhez in Tajikistan, Ashar and Asaba in Kyrgyzstan and Agzybirlik in Turkmenistan. Their protest ranged from the promotion of national languages and culture to calls for greater autonomy from Moscow and the centre, although very few groups demanded all-out secession.[9]

As the new freedom dawned, the Central Asian leaders quickly implemented many of the demands of the nationalist groups. During 1989-90, laws were passed to raise the language of the titular nationalists to the status of state languages and to ensure their greater use in public life. In the same period, declarations of sovereignty were announced and, following Gorbachev's example, the Central Asian party leaders transformed themselves into presidents. Although they remained loyal to the preservation of the Union, Karimov and Nazarbayev also went to great lengths to promote the interests of Central Asia and to show their constituencies that they were bargaining hard with the central authorities in Moscow.[10] By so doing, the Central Asian leaders successfully projected themselves as nationalist leaders, thereby undermining much of the popularity of the nationalist opposition.

The attainment of full independence at the end of 1991 further strengthened the nationalist credentials of the Central Asian leaders. The informal nationalist groupings had barely contemplated such unconditional independence. But one gain the Central Asian leaders made was that they received the lion's share of the reflected glory. The introduction of the trappings of statehood, new flag, constitutions, the opening of diplomatic relations, introduction into international organizations like the United Nations (UN) – all these were perfect public-relations opportunities for cementing their national and international stature. With effective control of the media, and with their connections to the mass of the population through the structures of power inherited from the Communist Party apparatus, the presidents of Central Asia had an unassailable advantage over the nationalist groupings, which were generally led by a city-based intelligentsia with only limited connection, or support from the countryside. What about Central Asia's Islamic inheritance and its impact on the concept of state and sovereignty? These questions need to be addressed briefly. Even in the many pilgrimages that Central Asian leaders may choose to make to Mecca, they are always likely to the viewed as communists or, more charitably, as secular nationalists.

It is partially a reflection of the uneasy relationship with Islam that the Central Asian leaders have consistently drawn a line between Islam as a private religion and Islam as a political force. Whilst permitting its growth as a religion, encouraging the building of mosques and the establishment of religious schools and training colleges, they have resisted any manifestation of a political voice for Islam. Thus, in Uzbekistan, Karimov was willing to register political opposition groups like Birlik and Erk, but refused to countenance the registration of an Uzbek branch of the Islamic Renaissance Party (IRP), which was established in Moscow as a Muslim democratic party. [11] In the other Central Asian states there has been a similar aversion to political bodies assuming a strongly Islamic identity and the ex-communist ruling elite has generally committed itself to the separation of state and religion (Islam).

Amongst the nomadic inhabitants of the Central Asian Steppe lands, Islam had a different historical development and its political power was never as fully formed or deeply embedded. The mosque as a stationary object was an alien intrusion on a society perpetually on the move.[12] The social structures of nomadic communities, which were generally free and less restricted than their sedentary counterparts, did not provide the ulema with the same moral authority. Also, many of the Kazakhs, the Kyrgyz and the Turkmen remained committed to more naturalist religious expressions, such as the Shamanist devotions to the natural environment. The late arrival of Islam and its less intensive intrusion into nomadic society meant that it remained more in the private than the public domain. As a politically mobilising force, Islam was only used if it had some practical advantage. When there was a direct threat from a non-Muslim source, such as the mass Russian immigration into Kazakh-Kyrgyz lands during the late nineteenth century, the banner of Islam was unfurled to mobilize opposition. However, when the threat came from fellow Muslims, such as the Kokand Khanates' intrusions into southern Kazakh lands, Islam played no role in the Kazakh defensive strategy.[13]

Taking into account the nomadic character of their societies in the past, in the originally tribal communities of Kazakhstan, Turkmenistan and Kyrgyzstan, the idea of a separation of Islam from politics is not so alien to their historical experience. Even as Muslim observance grows from its present very low levels, it is unlikely to develop a widespread political form.[14] So long as the ruling elite is sufficiently sensitive, there should be little cause for concern. Gestures such as Niyazov's pilgrimage to Mecca and Askar Akayev's confirmation of his oath of office on the Qur'an will probably continue to be sufficient.

Defence

In spite of intense Russification and Sovietization, Central Asia did not integrate into the Russian realm. On the basis of history and civilization, its identity remains as a prominent feature of emerging political and economic scenario. Nevertheless, the demise of the Soviet Union and the birth of independent Central Asian States brought them face to face with new problems or at least such problems as were not directly addressed by their respective governments. Many explosive issues came to fore, which had to be dealt with in an entirely new perspective. These, for example, are nationalism, sub-nationalism, ethnicity and along other fault lines like tribes and languages. Then there is the inter-state border issue, which may appear dormant for the time being, but is fraught with serious potential for a flare up at any given time. Ethnic tensions have not been new in the region. Such tendencies have already been manifest and have led to military conflicts, for example, between Armenia and Azerbaijan or between ethic groups in Ferghana valley. Political instability in Tajikistan and the fluid political situation in some parts of other republics could also be cited.

Speaking in terms of pressures likely to mount for military intervention in some Central Asian States, the basic question of how these states are going to meet the situation remains. And in fact, while speaking about defence implications, it is evident that each Central Asian state has to be treated on its merits because there are not identical situations as far as defence implications are concerned. Take the case of Tajikistan. Large numbers of Tajiks and Uzbeks live in the northern part of Afghanistan bordering Tajikistan. Ethnic affinity and rising Turkic nationalism have become poles of attraction for the Uzbek nationalities of Afghanistan. A movement led by the Uzbek guerrilla, Azad Beg, which is gaining support, calls for the Turkic people of Afghanistan, Uzbekistan and Turkmenistan to form independent Islamic states.[15] In the like manner, Tajiks project Ahmad Shah Masu'd, the Afghan Tajik ethnic leader who happened to be the Defence Minister in Rabbani government in Kabul. The concept of 'Greater Tajikistan' embracing the Tajiks of northern Afghanistan, as against the large mass of Turkic Muslims in Central Asia, particularly against the rising Uzbek nationalism, is also assuming serious dimensions. "Irredentism like this will not only pose a threat to Afghanistan, which is still torn by warring factions and ethnic rivalry but would also have a powerful effect on Central Asia on the lines of similar ethnic rivalry as well as Islamic fundamentalism through a spill-over effect from the southern frontier. On the request of the Central Asian Republics, the CIS reinforcements are defending the borders between Afghanistan and the Central Asian republics," writes Stobdan.[16]

The question of out-migration is likely to remain a continuous factor in Central Asian security. Currently between 150,000 to 200,000 Russians and other Europeans are leaving Central Asia every month. Population migration can have serious implications. In particular these implications can take a serious turn in republics where the Slavs are in sizeable strength. At the same time, these migrations might further activate right wing Russian nationalism with reactions to the Central Asian States. The trend of ethnic conflicts within Central Asia in the recent years show that there have been more cases of non-Russians killing non-Russians rather than ethnic Central Asians killing Russians.[17]

Uzbek nationalism is the most potent factor in the complex ethnic make-up of Central Asia. There have been numerous fights between the Uzbeks and Kyrgyzs. Uzbeks also fought Meshket Turks in Tashkent and the

Ferghana valley in 1983. Between Uzbeks and Tajiks, there has been perennial tension on the two Tajik-ethnicity areas of Samarkand and Bukhara. Not only do the Tajiks object to the idea of renaming Central Asia as Turkestan, as has been mooted by various quarters a number of times, but conflicts within Turkic sub-nationalities (Uzbeks and Kyrgyz) also indicate the likelihood of Pan-Turkism or Uzbek chauvinism taking shape in Central Asia. Not only do the Tajiks fear such a situation to surface, non-ethnic Central Asians in Central Asian republics are also apprehensive of such a development. It has already been said that there are still large numbers of Slavic people living in these states. The available figures are the following:

National composition of population in 5 Central Asia States is as follows:

Nationality	*1989*	*Percentage*
Uzbek	16,20,080	33.6
Kazakh	7,476,296	15.2
Tajik	4,162,524	8.5
Turkmen	2,672,174	5.4
Kyrgyz	2,482,210	5.1
Russian	9,516,229	19.4
Ukrainian	1,234,556	2.5
Tartar	1,178,698	2.4
German	1,134,097	2.3
Korean	320,189	0.7
Byelorussian	239,765	0.5
Uighur	258,952	0.5
Azerbaijani (Azeri)	187,273	0.4
Jewish	137,445	0.3
Armenian	111,064	0.2

Source: Robert J.Kaiser, 'Nations and Homelands in Soviet Central Asia' in *Geographic Perspective on Soviet Central Asia* (ed.) Robert A Lewis, Routledge, London, 1992, p. 289.

Islam

Central Asians have consistently drawn a line between Islam as a private religion and Islam as a political force. Whilst permitting its growth as a religion, encouraging the building of mosques and the establishment of religious schools and training colleges, they have resisted any manifestation of a political voice for Islam. Thus in Uzbekistan, Karimov was willing to register political opposition groups like Birlik and Erk, but refused to countenance the registration of an Uzbek branch of the Islamic Renaissance Party (IRP).[18]

The inherent difficulty of instituting a strict separation of state and religion is that conceptually it is contrary to Muslim tradition, and historically it has little precedence in the pre-Russian history of Central Asia. This is particularly the case in the sedentary oases settlement of Uzbekistan and Tajikistan, where Islam was especially pervasive and deeply embedded. These tightly knit communities accorded considerable respect and power to the Muslim clerics and the *ulema* who, in turn, defined the social, moral and political framework of their everyday existence. Bukhara's position as one of the leading religious centres of the Islamic world added to the fusion of spiritual and political power. The expansion of the Islamic Sufi orders (*tariqat*), like the Naqahbandiyya, Kubraviyya and Yasawiyya, which developed in the oasis towns of Central Asia, provided an ideology of universalism, which both cemented the political power of the sufi practitioners and increased popular devotion to Islam. In the nineteenth century, travellers to Bukhara, Khiva and Khokand vividly depicted the political and social power given to the *ulema* and dervish orders. At that time, the idea of a clear-cut division between state and religion was hardly comprehensible.[19]

Nationalism, and the crisis of identity it generated, affected another major factor in Central Asia, namely Islam. The Islamic revival in Central Asia has been quite an extraordinary and unprecedented phenomenon in the history of Islamic world and a clear rejection of the Soviet system. Nowhere in the world have religious feelings been suppressed for so long and with such brutality and yet been revived with such enthusiasm. There have been a number of distinct phases in this revival which, however, has spanned just five short years.[20]

The floodgates of the Islamic revival opened in 1989. It was a cultural, social and religious phenomenon, as people publicly wanted to demonstrate their separateness from the communist system and Slavic culture. Yet popular knowledge of the religion of Islam was minimal and information on political activism, ideas and debates in the Islamic world beyond Central Asia was almost non-existent.

Yet by 1992 in some areas such as Tajikistan and the Ferghana valley, the politics of Islam, generated in the Middle East and South Asia, was already being fought over with guns. Both the liberating aspects of the religion and culture of Islam and the unfortunate sectarianism that has plagued the Islamic world in the twentieth century arrived like a tornado in Central Asia.[21] The revival was exacerbated by the violent reaction to Islam of the ruling elite, who refused to understand what was happening or to accommodate it as part of their political agenda.

Gorbachev's *perestroika* and the loosening of communist control allowed the revival to take place. The impact of the defeat of the Soviet army inflicted by the mujahideen through a *jihad* - something that even the Basmachis had not achieved - created an even greater sense of awe and curiosity about Islam than might otherwise have developed. Above all, what emerged was a historical and cultural memory of the past even though its details were somewhat hazy. People learned to bypass official Islam as they set up their own mosques and other structures, while the arrival of funds, copies of the Qur'an (in millions), literature and mullahs from Saudi Arabia, Iran and Pakistan spread these countries' particular versions of Islam. The fundamentalist Muslim Brotherhood had long run a small underground movement through the Islamic Renaissance Party (IRP). The IRP was legalized in 1990 in Russia, but remained banned in Central Asia. The IRP and other Islamic groups had no compunction in declaring their intention to create an Islamic system in each republic which, they said, would lead to greater Central Asian unity. They considered both the ruling elite and the secular nationalists to be equal threats to this task.

Islam, Central Asia and the Region

The vacuum created by the lack of leadership from official Islamic hierarchy allowed fundamentalist groups to proliferate. The growing involvement of outside powers increased as Wahhabi groups from Saudi Arabia, Iranian Revolutionary Guards and some Sunni fundamentalist parties in Pakistan took advantage of the unprecedented political opportunity.[22] The refusal of Central Asian governments to allow Islamic education in government schools resulted in the spread of unofficial Islamic schools (*madrassahs*).

As a socio-political phenomenon, the emergence of political Islam in Central Asia cannot be understood separately from development in other parts of the Muslim world, particularly in the Middle East. This undercuts the widespread contention that the Central

Asian societies became so secularized during Soviet rule that they lost any strong Muslim identity. A recent case-study has shown that the Islamic resurgence in Tajikistan originated in the late 1970s and was mobilized by the Iranian revolution and the transnational propaganda of political Islam, just like Islamic movements in other regions of the Muslim World.[23]

The range of options open to the Central Asia secular nationalist leadership for dealing with the Islamist challenge similarly does not radically differ from that of their Middle Eastern counterparts. They can opt for repression as in Algeria or Egypt, they can seek to incorporate these Islamist groups in a democratic process as in Jordan or Yemen, or they can attempt to institute a conservative Islamic order as in Saudi Arabia. Repression is undoubtedly preferred option at present, but the other options could become potentially attractive at least in some of the states.

Islamic Central Asia and the West

Like the governments of Central Asia, the West, particularly the USA, also became unnecessarily hostile. During the Cold War, the Western powers had always used Islam as a means to undermine communism in Central Asia. In the 1920s, the British India supported the Basmachi with guns and money; again in 1939 the British infiltrated agents from Afghanistan and India to whip up Islamic feelings in Central Asia. Fitzroy Mclean, a British diplomat and secret agent, advised his government in a secret memorandum in October 1939 that Great Britain should help destabilise Central Asia using its mullahs in order to raise the bogey of Russia likely to invade Turkey and Iran, a lesson Germany had taught Britain.[24] In 1979, the USA used Islam in Central Asia to undermine communism. The CIA funded the Afghan mujahideen to smuggle millions of copies of the Qur'an, tape recordings, money and weapons to Islamic groups in Uzbekistan and Tajikistan.[25]

Yet after 1991, the West suddenly changed its stance. The US capital and international lending agencies entered Central Asia to play an important role. Thus, instead of supporting moderate Islam and legalizing Islamic parties, the rulers drove political Islam further to the wall, giving Islamic militants a propaganda ploy and every reason to accuse the rulers of being crypto-communists and unbelievers.

The spread of Islamic fundamentalism in Central Asia became a popular bogey in the Western media after the Tajik civil war began. However, as has been found, Tajik Islamists were driven as much by clan rivalries, the growth of localism and economic deprivations as by their desire to set up an Islamic state. Local people saw the IRP in Tajikistan as a political party first, representing the group interests of particular regions and clans, and an Islamic party second.[26] The fact that the IRP was allied to secular nationalist and democratic parties against the neo-communist forces appears to prove this. Similarly, in the Ferghana valley, it is the particular history of the valley and the present economic and political vacuum that has allowed fundamentalism to flourish there.

Since security concerns in Central Asia will be the main subject of the next chapter of this monograph, it may be said that the region will continue to be buffeted by competing international interests both economically and politically. While Russia and the West are trying to pull Central Asia away from the Islamic world, its Muslim neighbours are determined to build a greater economic and political consensus with the Central Asian states. Central Asia will also continue to be pulled in different directions by the dispute between the Arab world and Iran, between India and Pakistan and between Iran and Turkey. It still has major problems with Russia. All this will make any Central Asian unity much more difficult to realize.

There are no easy solutions to the problems of Central Asia. In the early twentieth century, this vast region had to cope with Russian colonization. Tsarism, revolution, civil war, famine, collectivisation and then ethnic nationhood and communism came one on the top of another.[27] More recently, it has had to deal with independence, breaking out of diplomatic isolation, economic hardship, ethnic conflict, a civil war in Tajikistan and the revival of nationalism and Islamic fundamentalism. The republics' leadership have so far just manage to keep their heads above water, preventing major economic and political chaos but unable to provide solution for an increasingly demanding and democratized public.

References

1. Milan Hauner, *What is Asia for Us? Russia's Heartland Yesterday and Today,* published by Unwin Hyman, London, 1990, p. 43.
2. Interview in *Moskovskye Novosti,* No. 15, Moscow, 12 April, 1993.
3. Interview in *Trud.* Moscow, 25 May 1993.
4. *Adephi Paper- 288, op. cit.,* p. 11.
5. Vaidyanath, R. *The Foundation of the Soviet Central Asian Republic*, New Delhi, 1990, p. 17.
6. Yasoav Rolin; *Central Asian Survey,* Vol. 10. No 9 London 1991. For a fuller analysis of the de-stabilizing consequences of the Central Asian delimitation, see Igor

Rotar 'The Bomb placed by the Kremlin Cartographers'. *Nezavisimaya Gazeta*, Moscow, 25 December, 1993.

7. *Adelphi Papers* - 188, *op. cit.*, p. 15.

8. For a fuller analysis of the different informal groups, see Shireen Hunter. 'Nationalist Movement in Central Asia', *Current History,* Vol. 89, no. 549, Washington, October 1990.

9. See James Critchlow.' Uzbeks Look Askance at Gorbachev's "Union" Ideas', *Research Report*, March, 1991.

10. For an analysis of the history and programme of the IRP, see Bess Brown.' The Islamic Renaissance Party in Central Asia.' *RFE/RL Research Report*, 10 May 1991.

11. *Adelphi Papers - 288* , *op. cit.*, p. 17.

12. The most detailed information on Islam's manifestations in the former Soviet Union can be found in Alexander Bennigson and S. Enders Wimbush, *Muslims of the Soviet Empire: A Guide*, London: C. Hurst, 1985.

13. R. Abazov, A. Vasilivetskil and V. Ponomarev, *Islam and Political Struggle in the CIS Countries*, Moscow, 1992 pp. 102 et seq.

14. *Newsweek*, 3 February 1992, p. 21.

15. P. Stobdan, 'Central Asian Regional Security', *Strategic Analysis*, Vol. XV. SV. No. 5, New Delhi, August 1992, p. 467.

16. *FSIS-Sov-92-081*, 27 April, 1992, p. 12.

17. Paul Goble, 'The Soviet Threat Revisited', *Ethncity and National Conflicts*, Ed. S. Neil Mack Farlane, Centre for International Relations, Queens University, Canada, *Rand Paper* 1992, p. 37.

18. See Bess Brown, ' The IRP in Central Asia', Research Paper WWW/W 10 May 1991.

19. *Adelphi Paper*-288, *op. cit.*, p. 7.

20. Ahmad Rashid, *The Resurgence of Central Asia*, *op. cit.*, p. 244.

21. *Ibid.*

22. *Ibid.* p. 245.

23. Allen Hetmanek, 'Islamic Revolution and Jihad Come to the Former Soviet Central Asia: the Case of Tajikistan', *Central Asian Survey*, Vol. 12, no. 3, 1993.

24. Authony Bevins, 'British Plot Aimed to Destabilise Soviets', *Independent*. 26 February 1990.

25. *The Resurgence of Central Asia, op. cit.*, p. 245.

26. See K.N. Pandita 'The Travails of Tajikistan', *The Pioneer*, New Delhi, 18 December 1995.

27. *The Resurgence of Central Asia, loc. cit.*, p. 251

CHAPTER IV

Russia and Central Asia: Security Concerns

Early Phase

De-colonised countries have generally formed their own guerrilla forces and liberation armies to defend their nascent independence. In most cases these groups were ultimately turned into regular armies to defend the new state and secure its border. The case of African National Army (ANA) can be cited as an example. But a de-stabilising factor about the five new Central Asian states was that none of these could guarantee its own security. With no regular armed forces of their own, they were forced to depend on the military forces of the former colonial power, i.e., Russia. Also, the goodwill of their neighbouring countries was needed to ensure their sovereignty.

A look at Central Asia in retrospect shows that on the eve of its independence from Russian control, it presented a picture of stark military contrasts. One of the five Central Asian states, Kazakhstan, became a *de facto* nuclear power state though not of her own volition but as a result of changed circumstances. This was bound to affect the nuclear balance of power. A significant thing was that this was a non-European or non-Western power. But as against it, in another state, namely Tajikistan, the growth of medieval-type of warlords and local militias led to a bloody civil war.

What happened in Tajikistan reminds us of the ongoing situation in Afghanistan. Yet one more country, Uzbekistan, began projecting itself militarily in the region not through its own military powers but by borrowing the military clout from Russia. One more Central Asian State, Kyrgyzstan unilaterally declared that she would neither build an army nor go in for nuclear weapons. The fact of the matter is that these states did not know how to meet the requirements of their security. Surprisingly, their leaders made no secret of the confusion that had overtaken them at the early stage of independence.

What were the parameters of strategic and military security, which could be threatened once Central Asian republics declared their independence from the Soviet Union? The foremost question was of the geographical borders. The existing borders had been carved out by Joseph Stalin in 1950s or even earlier. Widespread ethnic groups had made it practically difficult to carve out these states strictly on ethnic count. Ethnic nationalism and Islamic fundamentalism were two important factors which were bound to play a significant role in the future make-up of these states. The Russians, who managed the domination, were not sensitive to these factors.

It is well known that for more than a decade after the 1917 revolution, Central Asia was infested with violence by various groups at war with one another. White and Red armies, Basmachi militias, bandit gangs, mercenary nomadic cavalry units and foreign funded saboteurs stalked the Steppes and at will. Each tribal chief and regional satrap made his own claim to power through the barrel of a gun. If the control exercised by the central authority in Moscow were really decisive, then seventy years later one would not have seen the fearful scenario that surfaced in Tajikistan. That type of anarchy could spread to other states.

The security scenario of Central Asia at the time of dismemberment of the Soviet State was something like this. Moscow had exercised its multi-sided control of Central Asia through the Red Army Organisation called Turkestan Military District (TMD) with headquarters in Tashkent. It was an enormous military infrastructure, building roads, railways, telecommunication, depots, workshops and factories to help control one of the most volatile regions of the Soviet Union. Entire cities were constructed to house the military and then cordoned off from civilians. Later on, rocket factories and nuclear testing sites were added.

It is understood that TMD was created essentially to prevent the Muslim East from penetrating Soviet territory and to neutralize American encirclement of the Soviet Union from the south as the USA had built bases in Turkey, Iran and Pakistan. This was in addition to the military pacts. But when Beijing became the enemy, Moscow had to take cognizance of vulnerability of the long Sino-Russian border. The forces in Central Asia were turned around to face Chinese border. In 1979, TMD organised the invasion of Afghanistan and kept the 120,000 Soviet forces stationed there supplied for a decade. The Red Army became the crucible where race and religion were supposedly melted down to produce the new Soviet man.

Soviet Union collapsed, and the Red Army became the first target of ensuing chaos. Tens of thousands of its soldiers were demobbed as the new CIS armed forces took shape. Even in 1992, there were considerable CIS forces in Central Asia, nominally under the joint command of Russia and the respective republics in which they were stationed. Distribution of Central Asian forces at this point of time (1992) had been like this:[1]

Tajikistan	6,000	soldiers
Kyrgyzstan	8,000	
Uzbekistan	16,000	
Turkmenistan	34,000	
Kazakhstan	63,000	

In each of the Central Asian republics, the majority of conscripts were drawn from the republics, but many of the officers were Russian who had volunteered to stay on and serve in Central Asia. Some of them were to form the basis of the new republican armies.

Some data about the quantity of arms and ammunition which lay with these republics has been made available. According to this source, its details are like this:

Tanks	4,000
Armoured personnel	10,000
Artillery pieces	3,200
Aircrafts	220 [2]

Besides this, millions of small arms and huge underground ammunition dumps lay in the hands of these republics. De-stabilising at the centre could lead to these weapons falling into wrong hands. Later on, Tajik crisis revealed that many of the small arms including tanks fell into the hands of the bandits, local militia and the mafia chiefs. This apart, there was a very big question mark on the nuclear potential of Kazakhstan left behind by the Soviets. How was that going to affect the Central Asian, Russian, regional and international situation? This was a question which was being seriously discussed not only in Almaty, Moscow and other capitals in Central Asia but also in Washington and London.

Nuclear Issue

Kazakhstan's acquisition of nuclear weapons dominated Western and Asian strategic reactions to the Central Asian republics immediately after their independence. This republic had 104 SS-18 International Ballistic Missiles (ICBMs) with a total of 1,400 warheads on its soil. Each ICBM had a strike range of 11,200 kilometers and carried ten independently targeted warheads, each of which was equivalent to half a million tons of TNT. The two main missile bases were in the north, in areas dominated by Russian settlers. Overnight, Kazakhstan had become a nuclear power. It was a big responsibility for President Nursultan Nazarbayev and immensely disturbing for the world at large that barely knew him or his policies.

Americans were pursuing a non-nuclear policy for new entrants in the field soon after the Cold War ended. For them Kazakhstan was a new concern. Perhaps they failed to elicit a commitment form Moscow that Nursultan would not be an intransigent person. In August 1991, the coup to oust President Gorbachev failed. The US Secretary of State, James Baker, arrived in Alma Ata where President Nursultan told him that so long as Russia maintained its nuclear capability, Kazakhstan would retain its "nuclear weapons". "I am absolutely against having any single republic control all nuclear weapons by itself, irrespective of how large that republic might be. I say that in the Soviet Union defence should be unitary and all nuclear weapons should be under the control of central government," Kazakh President told Baker. In another meeting held in December of the same year, Nazarbayev told Baker that the nuclear inheritors of the Soviet State - Russia, Ukraine, Byelarus and Kazakhstan - should share the joint control of all nuclear weapons.[3]

On December 21, 1991, the formation of the CIS was formally announced. All the four nuclear states of the erstwhile Soviet Union agreed to keep the Soviet strategic arsenal under collective central command, accept US expertise in moving nuclear weapons from outlying republics to Russia by 1994 and carry out plans for the destruction of nuclear weapons. The only part of this agreement that was ever fulfilled was that by July 1992 all tactical nuclear weapons had been moved to Russia. The US Congress sanctioned payment of 400 million dollars to the four nuclear states for the destruction of their surplus nuclear weapons.

Ukraine and Kazakhstan now began politicising the nuclear issue. At the centre lay their sinister desire of extracting more and more concessions from Russia and greater financial aid from the USA. For some time of course, they did play their nuclear card very deftly. Nazarbayev, by any standard, began playing hide and seek. Sometimes he would show his cooperative stance but at other times he would adopt threatening postures. On January 28, 1992 he declared that he would not transfer his nuclear weapons to Russia. "It is not our fault that we have become a nuclear power," he told the French foreign minister Ronald Dumas.[4] At this point of time, when Nazabayev was bargaining on nuclear weapons disarmament programme, there were rumours afloat that Kazakhstan had sold one SS-18 to Iran and that it was about to provide Teheran with uranium. Veracity of such rumours can never be proved. No wonder, it could have been a part of the pressure tactics made use of by Kazakh President to extract more from Moscow and Washington.

START I Syndrome

In May 1992, a protocol was signed between President Nazarbayev and President George Bush in which Kazakhstan agreed to sign the first Strategic Arms Reduction Treaty (START 1), which would eventually allow the elimination of one-third of Soviet and US nuclear weapons. Ukraine and Byelarus had also signed such a protocol with the USA, so that all three states had guaranteed that they would either destroy their missiles or move them to Russia within seven days. All the three states pledged to sign the Nuclear Non-Proliferation Treaty (NPT) in the shortest possible time. Russia was officially designated as the successor nuclear state to the former Soviet Union. Once again Nazarbayev became ambivalent. "Our neighbour China is a nuclear power. Pakistan and India are nuclear powers. That is why we have clear position. It will take at least fifteen years to destroy these missiles if work progresses well. It would be desirable for these countries to join us," he said[5]. His stand had undergone a radical change. He was now demanding that all the neighboring countries of Kazakhstan with nuclear weapons should declare that they abandon these before Kazakhstan did so. It has made things more complicated though it had certainly made them more comprehensive in content and thrust.

START I was signed between the US and Russia in June 1992. According to this treaty, all land-based multiple warhead missiles were to be dismantled. The number agreed upon was that eventually each side would be fielding 3,000 to 3,500 warheads by the year 2000. The first missiles to be eliminated would be SS-18s, the very missiles on Kazakh soil. Ukraine, with 1,650 nuclear warheads on its soil, refused to fall in line and began a lengthy process of threats, blackmail and ultimatums to Washington and Moscow in a bid to obtain security guarantees from the USA and more than the 175 million dollars earmarked by Washington for Kiev for the elimination of its missiles. In January 1993, after three days of talks in Washington, Ukrainian leaders agreed to accept US security guarantees after Russia had agreed to compensate Ukraine for giving up its nuclear weapons.[6]

In May 1993, Ukraine again reneged on its earlier pledges and now renewed its demand of 3 billion dollars from the USA for dismantling its weapons. The US Defence Secretary, Les Aspin, made a visit to Kiev in June and engaged the sides in serious talks on the issue. He proposed that Ukrainian warheads be placed in storage under international supervision and that the US would help modernise Ukraine's conventional weapons systems.[7]

Analysts believe that no doubt Ukraine and Kazakhstan adopted a strategy of extracting as much as they could from Washington and Moscow, but in a way they had legitimate fears from Russia dominating the region. If Russia became the only Nuclear Weapon State in former Soviet Union, then these fears become more realistic. It was premised that uncertainty in Russia could bring a xenophobic leader to the surface there. Apart from this, a military coup could precipitate the use of nuclear blackmail to redraw its borders. Nazarbayev played a skilful game never appearing as stubborn as Ukraine, but using Ukraine's position as a stalking horse for his own policy.

Kazakhstan, NPT and Clandestine Sale

Washington was deeply committed to containment of nuclear warheads not only in Central Asia but also in the erstwhile republics of the Soviet Union and now the Russian Federation. Nazarbayev knew this. The new Clinton administration had placed non-proliferation at the top of its foreign policy agenda and could not afford to lose face at the hands of small republics whose international clout was minimal. The CIA chief, James Woollsey, told a Senate committee, "Non-proliferation is the most complex of challenges that intelligence community will face for the remainder of the century". He said that twenty-five countries were now developing nuclear, biological and chemical weapons and that some countries were trying clandestinely to obtain nuclear material from the former Soviet republics[8].

The West was indeed worried. Grapevine had it that Tajikistan was selling enriched uranium to potential Third World customers at the rate of $ 1000,000 for one kilogram. The Tajik government was now running a secret uranium plant near Khojend, but officials strongly denied that the plant was involved in illegal sales.[9] The plant had been built in the 1940s to provide fuel for the first Soviet atom bomb and had produced 3% or the former Soviet Union's total uranium.[10] In 1993, the US and Germany emphasised upon Kazakhstan the need of looking into the possible smuggling sale of low-grade nuclear fuel and metal such as beryllium and zirconium which are used in nuclear weapons. A report prepared by Russian foreign intelligence service and made public in the USA in 1993 cited "the growing interest of international organised crime structures in conducting illegal trade in fissionable and other especially dangerous material".[11] Notwithstanding these reports, the general assessment in international circles is that in the matter of nuclear materials, Central Asian republics have behaved with far greater sense of responsibility than expected after the collapse of the Soviet Union and they did not fall into the trap of temptation.

CIS, Central Asia and Security Concerns

Of other Central Asian States, it was Uzbekistan which expressed her concern about Kazakhstan's nuclear potential. President Islam Karimov felt that it threatened his clout because it jeopardized his bid to be the leader of the Central Asian group. He did not like western diplomats and officials visiting Alma Ata more frequently than Tashkent and providing Kazakhstan more aid than to Uzbekistan.

In the first year of independence, however, all the republics faced immediate problems of how to evolve effective security measures for their states. Immediately after the break-up of the Soviet Union, a Joint Military Command was set up in a bid to save the Soviet armed forces from disintegration. The six signatories of the agreement were Russia, Kazakhstan, Uzbekistan, Tajikistan, Kyrgyzstan and Armenia. Interminable negotiations between Russia and these republics about their future military relationship began. The crisis in the CIS military was acute. An eight-year restructuring plan was begun. Troops were demobbed and many of them faced return to Russia where housing, goods and money were in short supply. Morale amongst officers and men plummeted.

All this made it rather difficult for the CIS high command to formulate any new military doctrine. Without knowing how far their mandate stretched, it was difficult for generals to commit themselves to Central Asia. Initially, CIS troops in Central Asia were designated as part of CIS forces but were given a loose national status as they came under the joint command of officers from Russia and the respective republic. Even this arrangement was not entirely clear. Each republic negotiated for itself rather than following a joint Central Asian strategy. This only increased the chaos in the negotiations and delayed decisions.

The situation became more complicated in March 1992 when Russia said it would create its own army and defence ministry rather than rely on a united CIS force. For many Central Asian leaders this was a major blow, and forced even those leaders reluctant to do so to think about creating their own national forces. Almost immediately, Nazarbayev announced the setting up of a Kazakh National Guard. Uzbekistan said it would build a national army of 25,000 men, while Turkmenistan said it wanted no more than 2,000 men and would rely entirely on CIS forces.

At a meeting of Central Asian leaders in Beshkek in April 1992, President Nazarbayev proposed a common defence agreement amongst all the republics which could then be part of a large defence pact with Moscow, but this was turned down by President Islam Karimov of Uzbekistan. He, instead, proposed NATO-type local armies that would coordinate for a common defence. Turkmenistan refused to cooperate with other Central Asian States. Other leaders expressed their disillusionment with the CIS and said no military agreements could be made unless it was clear what the Russian army's role would be. Discussions on collective security arrangement quickly collapsed and no headway was made despite a number of Central Asian summits.

Joint Military Command Abandoned

In June 1993, the CIS formally abandoned the Joint Military Command set up in 1991 by Russia, Armenia and four of the Central Asian states. Russia, which would have had to bear the cost of such a command, refused to do so and the Central Asian states were left with the option of discussing a looser coordinating military body to be set up by 1994, or relying entirely on their own forces. The basic issues of defence thus remained unresolved as it was still not known how much coordination would be achieved. The questions were: what was to be the relationship between the CIS and the national forces? How were effective command and control structures to function and how were the division and maintenance of military hardware and facilities to be made?

Clearly two military doctrines needed to be meshed together; one based on the specific needs of each republic, and one for the CIS as a whole where Russian strategy would dominate. With Central Asian states in their infancy and Russia in turmoil, neither of the military doctrines could by created. A system of collective security was not workable because of the diverging security interests of the member states. Leaders still feared that the new CIS forces would only be a euphemism for the Russian army playing a colonial role in their republics. But in the first year after independence Russia appeared to withdraw from the region, not wanting to get sucked into hypernationalism, Islamic fundamentalism and economic breakdown that were prevalent.

Tajik Experiment

The Tajik civil war changed all that. Russia was soon providing help to Uzbekistan and the Tajik neo-communists to defeat the Islamic opposition. Russian military officers also realised that a landslide migration of Russians from Central Asia could trigger off a bloody reaction against Muslims in Russia itself and thus increase instability in the small autonomous Muslim Republics in Russia. And with its still significant Muslim population, Russia did not want to see the spread of Islamic fundamentalism into the territory. By 1993, she needed to contain the spread of fundamentalism from the south implying Iran, Afghanistan and Pakistan. That had become a truism in the CIS high command. Russia's defence minister, General Pavel Grachev, paid repeated visits to Tajikistan, raised the salaries of officers serving there and promoted many of them in the field.

The threat from Tajikistan was treated as a one-off event and did not bring the five republics closer in coordinating their military strategy. On the contrary, events in Tajikistan moved them further apart because the three smaller states became even more fearful than previously of Uzbekistan's political and military ambition. All the states except Kyrgyzstan, which refused to decorate an army, wanted their own national forces. But the expense involved in creating these was prohibitive and international lending agencies were in no mood to give loans to countries that would use already scarce funds to build armies. This problem must remain unresolved for the foreseeable future, although in the meantime Central Asian states have gone ahead in trying to form small national forces.

In 1992, Turkey quietly committed officer, men and equipment to Azerbaijan in its fight against Armenia. Iran could do the same if there was an appeal from some future pro-Islamic government in Tajikistan, while some officers in Pakistani military openly advocated a common defence pact between Pakistan and Central Asian states as a bulwark against India.[12]

Iranian Islamic Revolution and Soviet Muslims

As the Islamic factor is of considerable significance to the overall security concerns in Central Asia and Russia, it is only pertinent that one addresses the subject fully. And Islamic factor is presently greatly influenced by the Islamic revolution of Iran, a country with which Soviet Union had specific relations. The best approach to this part of the present study would be to try to understand the broad contours of Iranian Islamic revolution led by Ayatollah Khomeini, its regional impact and response in Islamic world and finally the revolution and the Muslims of the erstwhile Soviet Union.

Khomeini's Vision of Nationalism and Work Order

Led by men of religion, Iranian revolution was primarily against the ruling class. It enjoyed mass support before the actual take-over. The regime against which Khomeini worked was in some respects more closely akin to other "new" regimes in the Middle East than to the types of rule against which coup leader had risen elsewhere. Unlike other such regimes, the Shah's regime was monarchical and pro-Western, but like them it had come into existence after a military takeover, and it was reformist, modernizing, and secular to the point of being anti-clerical.

On every single count, Khomeini's ideology prescribed the opposite: the separation of religion and state was to be done away with, spiritual and temporal power to be united in the *velayat-e-faqih* (the rule of the jurisconsult); and foreign influence and the emulating of foreign role models to be halted. The Islamic ideology of Khumeini ignored the existence of political boundaries within the Muslim community. Khomeini's revolution sought to move Iran in the direction of Islamic *ummah* (community). The ideal of Hukumat-e-Islami was conceptualised by Khomeini while in exile. This concentrated on the theological-political questions regarding the *valayat-e-faqih*. The fault was that it did not offer any formula for the unification of the *umma*. Ethnic differences could not be just wished away, not to speak of sectarian divides within the Islamic community.[13]

On taking the office in August 1981, Mir Husayn Musavi, the foreign minister of the Islamic Republic of Iran declared, "One of the objectives of Iran's foreign policy was to carry the message of Iran's Islamic revolution to the entire world."[14] Ayatollah Miskhini, the Imam Jum'a of Qum, went to the length of saying that the goal of the revolution was "to impose the Quran over the entire world".[15] The moot point is whether the Islamic revolution was to be exported to Muslim countries through the use of force?

As for the more practical question of "exporting the revolution" to the Muslim world, the radicals had one advantage - they could point out that the very doctrine of *velayat-e-faqih* made it obligatory to do so whether for the ultimate purpose of the establishment of "the government of the Imam Mehdi" or for the more immediate need of making, "the Iranian regional environment safe for Iran's power and for its revolutionary ideology."[16]

But the more radical expressions regarding the "export" of the revolution typical of the early days were toned down over a passage of time. Khomeini himself had refrained from implying any intention to spread the revolution by force. The course of history, he stressed, made the spread of the revolution inevitable and irreversible. Iran need not "worm its way" into other countries, rather it should walk in "like an invited guest" - was the approach.[17] Early in 1984, Ayatollah Khomeini had said that his country wanted to show the Muslims what "correct Islam" really was. By then, the emphasis on "exporting" the revolution had clearly shifted to cultural ideological themes. As Foreign Minister, Ali Akbar Velayati put it: " It had nothing to do with exporting tanks and soldiers."

But some of Khomeini's associates were less restrained. They continued taking Khomeini's earlier views altogether literally because for many of them "exporting" the revolution was, and still is, a principal goal to be actively and constantly pursued by the Islamic Republic. Some of them continued to think and speak of him as the Imam for the Umma–the (spiritual and temporal) leader of the entire Muslim World. The 1984 Congress of Friday Imams resolved to accept Khomeini "as having the necessary qualifications for the Imamate of Muslims and we will invite Muslims to follow his call".[19]

It has to be remembered that in the case of Iraq, the Iranian revolutionary leaders had believed that Iraq should accept Imam Khomeini as the leader and follow the Imam and his line. But nowhere did it mean that Islamic Republic of Iran was exporting revolution through the use of arms - "we undoubtedly will not give direct aid to Muslim movements.... help them or to force them to change their regimes".

The Islamic Republic has a policy of not supporting such acts, and whatever is said about us to the contrary in this regard is untrue", affirmed Khomeini in 1984. Musawi stated similarly, "We do not want to export armed revolution to any country. That is a big lie. Our aim is to promote the Islamic revolution through persuasion". The Shi'i doctrine lays down that until the reappearance of the infallible Imam, the *vali faqih* can only lead a "defensive jihad". But then the term "defensive" is vague and flexible. The war against Iraq was viewed as a defensive war and some Iranians spoke of getting control of the holy cities in Saudi Arabia in order to "defend" Islam.

It will be noted that gradually there was a trend towards what Khomeini called the positive trend of nationalism according to which it was good to defend one's country. In July 1987, a leaflet was displayed in the Hajj pilgrimage. Such leaflets are usually representing the radical trends in Islam but Mehdi Karrubi, Khomeini's representative for the Hajj, spoke in this leaflet about ideological and emotional (*aqaidiyya* and *atifiyya*) foundations.

Iranian Islamic Revolution and Central Asia

Three sets of problems kept Iran preoccupied: the war with Iraq and Iran's isolation; the prolonged economic downturn and the growing domestic resentment and the power struggle within the revolutionary establishment. Together these posed a threat to the stability of the regime. Secondly, the initial failure in "exporting" the revolution has to be understood in a proper perspective. Khomeini and his men, when catapulted into the seats of power, firmly expected chain reactions in virtually all Muslim societies. One of Khomeini's Arab correspondents said, "be patient ... we will both see the fate of Saudi rulers six months after our return to Iran".[20]

But contrary to the expectations of the revolutionaries in Iran, the Muslim world continued keeping its cool. In 1985, the Prime Minister of Iran made much more sober assessment saying, "Initially our view regarding exporting the revolution was that the Islamic revolution would spread within a year as a chain reaction. This idea is not altogether unrealistic in the long run. But it seems that we were wrong in our initial assessments with regard to the fast spread of the revolution".[21]

In conclusion, it will be seen that after 1985, the fervour for export of Islamic revolution began giving way to reformed nationalism in Iran. The expected spontaneous and widespread acceptance of the Iranian revolutionary example has not materialised. The export of revolution had to give way to consolidation of the revolution in Iran as an attractive example to be emulated elsewhere. A new form of Iranian territorial identity is being promoted in practice. Khomeini's perception of Iranian identity saw Islam as the decisive cohesive element but the exigencies of realpolitik could not be lost sight of. Therefore, while the fervour of "export" of Iranian revolution had substantially subsided by 1985, the collapse of the Soviet Union started in 1991. By that time, the strength and influence of Iranian revolution, which could have accounted for a sensational turmoil within Central Asia, had receded into background. It will be pertinent to briefly consider the impact of Iranian Islamic revolution on Central Asia in order to assess the importance of the factor of Islam in the security formulations of Central Asian States.

Iranian Revolution and Central Asian Muslims

As early as 1980, Iranian reactionaries spoke for the need of strong bridges to link them with Soviet Muslims. Khomeini and spokespersons of his regime had made it clear that they regarded the USSR's Muslims as natural targets for Iranian propaganda and religious activity.[22] A decade later, a reputed Russian orientalist, Igor Beliaev asserted in an article entitled 'Khomeini: A Political Portrait' that the Iranian leaders' dream was for the Islamic revolution to be victorious throughout the entire Muslim world from Moscow to Indonesia. He considered the Soviet Muslim areas as included in this. Indeed, Jalalal-Din Farsi, a candidate (later disqualified) in the 1980 Iranian Presidential election, had told Beliaev in 1981 that following the Shi'i revolution in Iran, there would be a second Sunni one in Afghanistan and a third one in the Soviet Union.[23] To be fair to Beliaev, the second prediction has already come true.

Though communist administration at that point of time discounted impact of Iranian revolution on the people in Central Asia, but on the ground one could feel that the impact was substantial. In Baku (Soviet Azerbaijan), the Muslim elders of the city sent a congratulatory telegram to Khomeini when he took over. Taxi drivers played Iranian music. Local Muslims complained of scarcity of mullahs and also of copies of the holy Qur'an. They accused Russian minority of dominating the republic's life. Shortly after the Iranian revolution, a rural inhabitant of Azerbaijan wrote to the journal *Nauka Religiia*, "we in Azerbaijan are all very happy about the Iranian revolution, for it has shown the entire world the greatness of Islam. This religion should be introduced among us, too, as obligatory; then everything will be in accordance with the laws of purity and integrity, whereas now, when Islam is forgotten, there is in our ranks much deceit and filth".[24]

Undoubtedly, the authorities were concerned. In late 1980, both the first secretary of Azerbaijan communist party and politburo candidate member Geidar Aliev, and the head of the republican KGB, Zia Yusuf Zadeh, called for effective security measures in view of the Iranian events.[25] In Turkmenia, another Soviet republic bordering Iran, the population was reportedly listening regularly to religious broadcasts from Iran in Turkmen. These were said to be recorded on tape and played back by mullahs before groups of believers throughout the republic, especially in the areas more distant from Iranian frontier, where the broadcasts could not be heard directly. By 1987, Iran was beaming several hours of daily broadcasts for the Soviet Union, as well as television programme to disseminate material of an Islamic nature. Moreover, many inhabitants were receiving letters from Iran supposedly from relatives consenting to perform the Haj in their name and suggesting that the recipients should also persuade fellow villagers to make the Hajj by proxy and organise alms-giving (*sadaqa*), prayer meetings and other actions contrary to Soviet law. A further indirect indication of the prevalence of Iranian propaganda materials was included in the report of an Uzbek language newspaper in 1986 to the effect that the Tashkent Customs authorities had won second place in an All Union competition among departments of the main administration for State Customs Inspections of the USSR Council of Ministers. They had to contend with numerous attempts to bring in narcotics, valuables, currency and ideologically harmful materials.[26] There can hardly be any doubt that allusion is to materials from Iran.

In the spring of 1987, Igor Beliaev wrote a lengthy article in the influential paper of the union of writers, *Literaturnate Gazeta*, entitled 'Islam and Politics', which opened with a letter from a student asking whether it was true, as western politicians believe, "that Soviet Muslims were subjects for the influence of their co-religionists in other countries" who were conducting an unflagging struggle against socialism? Instead of giving a direct respnse, Beliaev preferred to discuss the rise of Islamic fundamentalism outside the Soviet Union and look at the strength of Islam within the country. While not committing himself to the actual existence of an Islamic opposition inside the USSR, Beliaev did concede that "Muslim fanatics and Sufis" had manipulated the youngsters into participating in the Alma Ata disturbances of December 1986 following the dismissal of Kazakh SSR Party Secretary. Dinamukhamed Kunaev. Beliaev cited the late French expert on the Soviet Muslim community, Alexander Benningsen, for the view that Sufi propaganda was constantly increasing among Soviet Muslims, and that an "Islamizdat" i.e. Muslim *samizdat* (unofficial uncensored literature) existed which included printing and xeroxed writings on religious themes and disseminating tapes with passages from authoritative and sacred Muslim texts.

Nor was Benningsen alone in the field. A scholar at the West German Bundesinstitut Fur Ostwissenschaftliche also believed that Iranian developments influenced the USSR's Muslims belongingness and self-consciousness, as well as actual religiosity.[27]

Assessing the Impact

Undoubtedly, Khomeini wanted to bring his radical Islamic message to his Soviet co-religionists and these materials embodying a resurgent Islamic ideology were reaching the Soviet Muslim population from Iran. The increasing strength of Islam in Central Asia had been drawing attention in Moscow as well as in the West some time prior to the Iranian revolution. Islam had undoubtedly rendered certain Soviet Muslim sectors receptive to its call. In September 1987, at a seminar held in Makhachakale (in Dagestan ASSR) on ' Islam in Contemporary Society: Political, Economic and Moral Aspects', three main factors were cited as promoting the continued prevalence of Islam in the Central Asian republics and various regions of the Russian Soviet Federal Socialist Republic. These were the pervasiveness of religious propaganda, the ineffectiveness of atheistic activity, and the influence of foreign radio broadcasts.[28] An all-Union scientific theoretical conference entitled 'Islam and Politics' was held in Dushanbe in May 1988, attended by orientalists, Turcologists, philosophers and economists from

Moscow, Leningrad, Erevan and the republican capitals of Central Asia and, of course, from the Tajik SSR. These scholars had previously been focusing their attention on current developments in the East "where Islam has for a number of national and historical reasons played a great role and in places where Islam is the official religion." Radio Dushanbe declared, "Its propaganda apparatus has been organised very well and its activities have also influenced neighbouring regions in the Soviet Union."[29] In April 1987, another conference was held in London (the Second European Seminar on Central Asian Studies, ESCAS II). Soviet scholars admitted in answer to a question that Middle Eastern Islamic movements might have some impact on their own 'Islamic regions'.[30] In individual cases, Iranian propaganda seems definitely to have had some direct influence. A pensioner in Turkmen republic admitted before a rural assembly that he had begun vigorous religious activity under the immediate influence of Iranian broadcasts. In Tajikistan, a 'wandering mullah' was charged with inciting people to religious zeal. According to a court document in 1985, this man had told a gathering of some twenty-five to thirty people that on the previous evening, he and a few devout Muslims had listened to the Iranian radio and heard a prominent Iranian cleric calling on all Muslims to unite under the banner of Islam.

In the same republic there were said to be several dealers in illegal religious literature. These materials included an illegally published newspaper *Islamskaya Pravda*, photocopies of speeches by Khomeini and a Pakistan political leader, books by Jamalu'd-Din Afghani, a major theorist of Islamic revival, and works by the founder of the Muslim Brotherhood, Hasan Banna, and other Muslim Brotherhood theoreticians. One dealer in religious *samizdat* (illegal literature) obtained some of his material from Osh Oblast in Kyrgyzia. Other literature had been obtained locally, while the police had uncovered the membership in a distribution centre connected with Baku of an external student at the Dushanbe Pedagogical Institute who had used the institute's printing shop to produce 12,000 flyers with religious texts and some religious brochures.[31]

Moreover, as *Turkmenskata Iskara* had pointed out, it was not only individuals who were "deceived". The green banner of Islam and pictures of Khomeini were held high by demonstrators not only in Alma Ata in December 1986, but also in Baku in November 1988, in connection with the disturbances that shook the Azerbaijan SSR over, and in the wake of, the Nagorno Karabakh dispute with its Armenian neighbour.[32] In Baku, too, demonstrators were wearing the red headband, which in Iran is a symbol of holy martyrdom and worn by soldiers going off to the war with Iraq.[33] The banners and photos of Khomeini were also noticed at demonstrations in Dushanbe in February and March 1989 and in the eastern part of Uzbekistan in June 1989.

There has been some dispute among Soviet experts as to the forces motivating the nationalist uprising in the first half of 1989 in Central Asia and Kazakhstan. While one school of thought attributes them solely to socio-economic forces, others have suggested that religious and nationalist factors have played a meaningful role. Certainly, today no one would deny the existence of major social and economic problems in the area: large-scale unemployment, a visibly deteriorating health situation, a dearth of housing and serious ecological problems.

In this atmosphere, religious fanaticism has also been a factor. Just prior to the disturbances in Ferghana

Oblast, "hooligans" were reported to be intimidating Uzbek women and forcing them to dress and behave in accordance with Islamic law.[34] *Moscow News* listed among the reasons for discontent in Eastern Uzbekistan the fact that in the whole of Ferghana valley there was only one working mosque.[35] Lt. Gen. V.K. Pankin, head of the USSR Interior Ministry's Main Administration for Criminal Investigation, told a Tass correspondent that the riots in Ferghana valley were unquestionably pre-planned, that members of the unofficial Uzbek National Front, Birlik were active in them and that the demonstrators' slogans included: "Hail the Islamic banner, the Muslim religion and Ayatollah Khomeini."[36]

The same paper that carried the interview with Pankin said elsewhere that Muslim underground organisation in Uzbekistan disseminated pamphlets directed against Russians Armenians, Jews and Tartars, warning these "infidels" to leave the republic. The reference to Tartars may be to the Volga Tartars who comprise the largest non-Uzbek ethnic groups in Tashkent after the Russians. They are traditionally Muslims but are generally secular and modernist.

Islam as a Factor in Central Asian Security

Gorbachev's *perestroika* and the loosening of communist control allowed the revival to take place. The impact of the Afghan Mujahideen's victory over the Soviet army through a jihad — something the Basmachis had not achieved—created an even greater sense of awe and curiosity about Islam than might otherwise have developed. Above all, what emerged was a historical and cultural memory of the past even though its details were somewhat hazy - that Central Asia had been the home of vast Islamic empires that once ruled Russia and the world. At their own expense people rushed to build mosques and hire young mullahs to teach them the tenets of Islam. The bureaucratic structure of official Islam, that is Islam sponsored by the state, was swamped by public in Central Asia. It had ignored these demands and failed to modernize, fund or support the official Islamic bureaucracy. There were a series of revolts by the public against the Islamic hierarchy and a number of Islamic clerics were thrown out of office after being accused of being communists, alcoholics or womanisers.

People learned to bypass official Islam as they set up their own mosques and other structures, while the arrival of funds, copies of the holy Qur'an, literature and mullahs from Saudi Arabia, Iran and Pakistan spread particular versions of Islam of their respective countries. The fundamentalist Muslim Brotherhood had long run a small underground movement through the Islamic Renaissance Party (IRP). The IRP was legalized in 1990s in Russia, but it remained banned in Central Asia. The IRP and other Islamic groups had no compunction in declaring their intention to create an Islamic system in each republic which, they said, would lead to greater Central Asian unity. They considered both the ruling elite and the secular nationalists to be equal threats to this task.

The vacuum created by the lack of leadership from the official Islamic hierarchy allowed fundamentalist groups to proliferate. The growing involvement of outside powers increased as Wahhabi groups from Saudi Arabia, Iranian Revolutionary Guards and some Sunni fundamentalist parties in Pakistan took advantage of the unprecedented political opportunities. The refusal of Central Asian governments to allow Islamic education in government schools resulted in the spread of unofficial Islamic schools or *madrasahs*.

Like the government of Central Asia, the West, particularly the USA, became unnecessarily hostile. During the Cold War, the Western powers had always used Islam as a means to undermine communism in Central Asia. In the 1920s, the British in India supported the Basmachis with guns and money. Again in 1939, the British infiltrated agents from Afghanistan and India to whip up Islamic feelings in Central Asia. Fitzroy Mclean, a British diplomat and secret agent, advised his government in a secret memorandum in October 1939 that British should help destabilise Central Asia using its mullahs in order to prevent Russia invading Turkey and Iran as Germany fought Britain.[37] In 1979 the USA used the Afghan war to spread Islam in Central Asia and undermine communism. The CIA funded the Afghan Mujahideen to smuggle the copies of holy Qur'an, tape recordings, money and weapons to Islamic groups in Uzbekistan and Tajikistan.[38]

Yet after 1991 the West suddenly changed its tactics. The US Secretary of State, James Baker, publicly warned Central Asian leaders to stay clear of radical Islam and the influence of Iran. This only encouraged Central Asian leaders increase their rhetoric against fundamentalism in order to gain audience in Western capitals and international lending agencies. Thus, instead of supporting moderate Islam and legalising Islamic parties, the rulers drove political Islam further to the wall, giving Islamic militants much-needed propaganda ploys and every reason to accuse the rulers of being crypto-communists and unbelievers.

The spread of Islamic fundamentalism in Central Asia became a popular bogey in the Western media after the Tajik civil war began. However, Tajik Islamists were driven as much by clan rivalries, the growth of localism and economic deprivation as by their desire to set up an Islamic State. Local people saw the IRP in Tajikistan as a political party first, representing the group interests of particular regions and clans, and an Islamic party later.

Tajikistan is a special case in dealing with religion and security question in Central Asia. It is Tajikistan alone among the independent republics of erstwhile Soviet Union where an open armed confrontation between the radicals and the ruling groups took place. Additionally, Tajikistan's borders touch those of Afghanistan to her south. Afghanistan has undergone great turbulence while fighting the Russian incursion. The aftermath of the Soviet withdrawal has been traumatic for Afghanistan and the country is at war with itself. That Afghan fundamentalism spilled over to Tajikistan is also given due importance by some observers. Be that as it may, the fact remains that Tajikistan has put to severe test the security efforts of Russian Federation and other members of the security group in CIS. Essentially, the joint resistance at the Tajik-Afghan border is against the fundamentalist forces but in the process and as a fall-out of Afghan war, actual armed confrontation has been taking place. If Tajikistan succumbs to the religious extremists at home and from abroad (essentially Afghanistan), then the entire security scenario of Central Asia will undergo a radical change.

In the past five years, Tajikistan has lived through *coup d'etats*, change of presidents and government, and civil war. It is typical that the participants' long meetings in city squares, those who capture deputies as hostages, and rebel against government, all pursue one aim — personnel shifts. So what we witness in that republic is an onslaught of the radical Islamists, feudal internecine discord and war of regional clans.

The prevalent opinion is that the sides in the confrontation are government troops and the Tajik opposition. But deployed in the country is also the Russian rifle division 201 and a group of frontier units as well as battalions from Kyrgzya, Kazakhstan and Uzbekistan, who guard the segments of the Tajik-Afghans border assigned to them. 201 Division, which in 1992- 93 took part in the armed action against the Tajik opposition, is now called a peace unit. In fact, the combatants are the Russian frontier troops and the opposition, although Russia is also involved as a go-between in the peace talks between the opposition and the Dushanbe government. As far as the battle-worthiness of the government troops is concerned, Russian experts say it is low. The defence ministry is eroded by corruption and power struggle among the higher-ranking officers, and the servicemen disperse after the first encounter with the enemy.[39]

The opposition's strategic objective is to return home and gain a legitimate status. Proceeding from this, the unit of Tajik opposition located in northern Afghanistan operates in two main directions, military and diplomatic. Not infrequently, the opposition uses hostilities to pressurise the official Dushanbe government into concessions during the talks. The objective of Tajikistan's leadership is to preserve the status quo and prevent the opposition members from coming back home. These in-depth distinctions in the principal goals make it impossible for the sides to develop a common stand and reach national accord.

Confrontation with the opposition is a derivative of the main problem. There are five regions on the political map of Tajikistan. This was the traditional scheme accepted as given by the Central authorities.

The republic's leaders used to be recruited from the economically advanced Leninabad Oblast (north), which had the top place in the hierarchy of Tajikistan's regions. However, after the Soviet Union fell apart, the first crack appeared in this arrangement: southern Tajiks claimed more rights for themselves.

President Rahaman Nabiev, a native of Leninabad Oblast, resigned under the pressure of the armed opposition, and his duties passed over to Akbarsho Iskandarov, a southerner. However, in late 1992, the Islamic democratic government fell, and the Popular Front, whose backbone was constituted by natives of Kulyab Oblast, pushed the opposition into Afghanistan. That was a war of southerners against southerners, which should have led to the Northerners' revanche. However, the executors gained control over the situation, and there began mass-scale Kulyabization, which angered yesterdays' allies, natives of Hissar and Leninabad Oblast.[40]

Who should rule the republic, and what should be the regional representation in the power structure? These and other serious questions have come to the fore. As in neighbouring Afghanistan, the formation of a political elite promoting national and not narrow and ethnic interests is a condition of peace and stability. If the regional leaders fail to reach agreement, Tajikistan may disappear from the map of the world, falling into zones of influence of large states. This is a glimpse of internal security concern of the Republic of Tajikistan.

Without question the first fiddle in Tajikistan is played by Russia, which injects loans and military aid into its ally. The present government and President Rahmanov came to power with the support of Moscow and Tashkent. However, in the past two or three years the alignment of forces has changed quite dramatically.

Two geopolitical axis were formed; Dushanbe - Moscow, Ashkabad - Teheran - Tashkent. Tajik opposition thinks Moscow is trying to protect the pro-Russian leadership of Tajikistan; Tashkent (with Bishkek and Alam-a Ata siding with it) is advocating a compromise between Dushanbe and the opposition. Tashkent would like the Dushanbe government to remain loyal to Uzbekistan and to keep the latter's interests in mind. The worst possible scenario is Afghanisation of Tajikistan. If that happens then the regions bordering on Uzbekistan could become a buffer zone and fall under the control of the powerful neighbour.

Ever since the outbreak of the conflict, this ideology has serviced the internecine war. Leninabad ruled under a red banner. The southerners used Islamic and democratic political lingo, although the fundamental idea was national revival. The present leadership, after it came to power under the red banners, discarded the communist jargon. It failed to produce a new attractive ideology. Dushanbe still waving the much worn flag has the threat of Islamic fundamentalism inscribed on it. In the meantime, *coup d'etats* may keep recurring, pushing forward different combinations of insurgent commanders until compromise between region and clans is reached,. The events in Kyrghyzstan, Uzbekistan, and Kazakhstan show that the same rule is applicable.[41] For the time being unstable peace exists in Tajikistan.

Security in Global Strategy

The contemporary internal significance of the new Central Asian States reflects their economic and demographic potential, geographical location, the character of their relations with other states, primarily with neighbouring ones, as well as their role in regional and global international organisations. Over fifty-five million people live in the region of former Soviet Central Asia, which is quite rich in natural resources as well as in terms of its economic, scientific and technological potential.

The strategic significance of the region derives from the fact that it borders two of the five nuclear states of the world — Russia and China — and through Iran and Afghanistan it has access to the Persian Gulf and Indian Ocean. With the completion of trans-Asian railway projects and the development of road and air communications, the geo-strategic trade and economic significance of Central Asia will rise further, for it will start to serve as a route for considerable cargo flows from Asia and the Pacific region to Europe and West Asia as well as from the west to the east.

Political and Military Threats

The official documents on military policy of the Central Asian States (CIS) do not specify probable enemies, although CIS documents signed by these states suggest in broad terms the sources of potential military danger.

In October 1993, Kazakhstan, Kyrgyzstan, Uzbekistan and Tajikistan signed in Bishkek an agreement on the concept of military security of the CIS member-states. This document considers the instability of the social, economic, military and political situation in a number of regions, the existence of potential in certain states which exceed their defence needs, the proliferation of nuclear and other weapons of mass destruction, "as a major source of potential military threat for member-states of the CIS.[42]

At a summit meeting of the CIS in February 1995, a declaration of member-states on the collective security agreement and a concept of collective security were adopted. This concept, which of course was not meant to apply only to the Central Asian region (Turkmenistan has not signed the original collective security agreement), defines major sources of military danger and factors which might contribute to military dangers evolving into a direct military threat as follows:

- The buildup of military capabilities in the region's neighbouring member-states to limits that disturb the existing balance of forces
- The formation and training in the territory of other states of armed forces intended for use against member-states.
- Inflaming border conflicts and armed provocation from the territory of bordering states.
- The transfer of foreign troops into territories neighbouring the member state (if this is not connected with peace-keeping measures in accordance with the resolutions on the UN Security Council or CSCE.

However, a significant handicap for the Central Asian States (CIS) is the fact that their armed forces are still at the initial stages of formation. They are fragments of the collapsed armed forces of the former Soviet Union, and, therefore, do not yet have a single internal system, which includes command and control, communications, a comprehensive supply system, mobilization readiness, the training of personnel and defence production. Despite this, after independence,the Central Asian States have determined the general structure of their armed forces. Command and control bodies, military doctrines and military policies as a whole are being worked out.

China Factor

Does a military threat to Central Asian States arise from regional states beyond the CIS region such as China, Afghanistan, and Iran? Among the latter, only China has a powerful military potential, which includes nuclear weapons. The Lanchzhou military district bordering Central Asia is the fourth largest Chinese military district where twelve Chinese land divisions are deployed. The Lop Nor nuclear test site is also situated in the same district.

Referring to a seminar organised by the Rand Corporation in Almaty in October 1992, S. Kurginian maintained in *Nazavisimaya Gazeta* that "Lanchzhou military district, if aimed directly at Kazakhstan, can deploy about 400,000 soldiers, 500 tanks, 3,000 artillery pieces and mortars, and 480 aircraft in the event of a conflict." He argued that "the 40th Afghan army, which was left as a legacy to Kazakhstan from the Soviet forces deployed in the republic, would not be sufficient even to guard together more or less effectively".[43] This analysis noted not only the increasing military force of China, but also unsettled border issues and a form of ethnic expansion – the infiltration of Chinese into other countries for permanent residence.[44]

Another part of the myth about the "Chinese threat" is that Beijing can accuse the Central Asian states of allowing their territories to be used by some Uighur organisations for subversive activities against China.[45] Both in the Russian and Western press, a number of publications have reported that the appearance of newly independent states in Central Asia stimulates the struggle of Turkic-Muslim peoples in China, mainly Uighurs, for their national independence.

Pan-Turkic/Pan-Islamic

However, in Central Asia there are no signs of any pan-Turkic or pan-Islamic solidarity. The Central Asian States maintain the principle of non-interference in the internal affairs of other States and do not permit any organisations to undertake activities which would damage their relations with other states, including China. The registration of such an organisation is not permitted and their activities are prohibited.

The leaders of Russia signed an agreement on strengthening confidence-building measures in the military areas at the end of April 1996 in Shanghai. China, Kazakhstan, Kyrgyzstan and Tajikistan were of particular significance in enhancing stability and developing neighbourliness between these states. The agreement stipulated the withdrawal of armed forces and armament, except border forces, from zone 100 kms. from the border, the cessation of military exercises directed against the other side, and limitations on the size and number of forces participating in military exercises as well as the need for the states to inform each other about such exercises. It also established friendly relations between the border troops and provided for the mutual invitation of observers to military exercises.

Iran

Iran, which ranks as the second world oil state after Saudi Arabia and raises about $ 20 billion a year from oil sales, has considerable armed forces and is conducting a large scale programme of rearmament. Western states accuse Iran of creating an infrastructure for the production of nuclear weapons, mainly with the assistance of China. However, it may be said with reasonable confidence that Iran is not and will not become a source of military threat to the Central Asian States. Iran is increasing its military potentiality in order to become a major regional power centre in the Persian Gulf. This is a long-term goal of its external policy, and notwithstanding the fact that Iran has interests in the northern and northeastern perimeter of its border - Trans-Caucasia, Central Asia and Afghanistan. The lessons of the Iran-Iraq war suggest that Iran will not use force, let alone armed aggression against any of its neighbours, at least in the foreseeable future.

Afghan Spillover

The real threat to the security of newly independent states of Central Asia is the situation of the Tajik-Afghan border, which poses the danger of 'Afghanistanization' to Central Asia – the possibility of the new Central Asian States cracking at their "ethnic seams" as it is occurring in Afghanistan. This could follow if the Tajik-Afghan border were to disappear and Iran, Pakistan, Russia and Uzbekistan, the states bordering and involved in Afghan affairs, declare their interest in the integrity of Afghanistan, since its fragmentation could become a serious source of destabilization in and around the region.

The fracturing of the CIS (Central Asian States) along ethnic lines is a potential danger for Russia itself since, as noted by Russian analysts, this region forms the 'soft underbelly' of Russia. In response Russia would have to build new state borders in an attempt to contain what is viewed as 'Islamic fundamentalism'.

Yet neither Russia, nor the Central Asian states are able to equip new intra- CIS State borders between themselves. According to Russian estimates, the equipment of one kilometer of border would cost not less than one billion roubles. The decision whether to continue to guard the 1400-km long Tajik-Afghan border, or to leave Tajikistan and to start the construction of a new 6200-kms long Russian-Kazakh border is a serious issue for Russia. But it is influenced by the fears noted above and by the fact that the Central Asian States themselves cannot afford the constructing and equipping of new state borders. Therefore, it is in the interests of Russia and the Central Asian states to leave 'transparent' border between themselves, but to strengthen the protection of outer borders of the CIS, especially the Tajik-Afghan sector.

It is in Russian's strategic interests to strengthen the state sovereignty and territorial integrity of the Central Asian states, promote the development of the economic and defence potential of the Central Asian States and engage in military and political cooperation in order to protect the common borders of the CIS by means of joint forces. A coincidence of strategic interests underlies the treaties of friendship, cooperation and mutual assistance signed by Russia and Central Asian States. These treaties presuppose mutual defence obligations in the event of aggression against any one of the parties. Similar interests underpin more specific treaties on military cooperations. In order to be more precise in regard to security concerns of Central Asia, it would be proper to deal with individual states in order to frame a total overview of the situation.

Kazakhstan

The backbone of the defence policy of the Republic of Kazakhstan may be summarised as follows:

Firstly, the formation of Kazakh armed forces capable of defending the sovereignty and territorial integrity of the country is underway. Secondly, in May 1992, Kazakhstan and Russia concluded an agreement on Friendship, Cooperation and Mutual Assistance, by which they reiterated to render each other military assistance in case of aggression against one of them. A supplementary agreement on military cooperation was signed together with a package of documents on military issues. Russia is leasing the Baikonur space facility. There remain forces and military sites on the territory of Kazakhstan under Russian jurisdiction. Thirdly, Kazakhstan signed in May 1993 a CIS collective security treaty and is making every effort to create a joint defence space aimed at the coordination of defence activities with CIS partners.

One of the important factors reinforcing the security of Kazakhstan after it joined the nuclear Non Proliferation Treaty (NPT) as a non-nuclear state was the acceptance of formal affirmation of security from Russia, the Unites States and Great Britain. In December 1994, during the CSCE summit in Budapest, Presidents Yeltsin and Clinton and Prime Minister John Major signed the Memorandum of Security Guarantees. They confirmed their commitment to respect the independence, sovereignty and existing borders of Kazakhstan, and to avoid the use of force against the territorial integrity or political independence of Kazakhstan, as well as to avoid exerting economic pressure against her.

If Kazakhstan becomes a victim of aggression or an object of nuclear threat, then Russia, the US and UK will demand immediate action from the UN Security Council to render assistance to Kazakhstan as a non-nuclear state of the NPT. The Chinese government has also offered Kazakhstan guarantees of security. As expressed by the Xinhua agency on 8

February 1995, " China fully understands the desire of Kazakhstan to obtain security guarantees, to abstain unreservedly from the use of nuclear weapons or the threat of their use against non-nuclear states and non-nuclear zones. This is the consistent position of the Chinese Government. This position of principle applies to Kazakhstan.[45]

The Armed Forces

When the Soviet Union was dissolved in December 1991, the armed forces on the territory of Kazakhstan consisted of 4,40,000 military personnel. About 95 per cent of the officers were from Russia, Ukraine and Byelarus. When Russian President Yeltsin created the armed forces of the Russian Federation, President Nazarbayev expressed a clear preference for the preservation of unified CIS forces. Consequently, the process of separating Russian, CIS and Kazakhstan armed forces was undertaken. The World War II veteran Sagadata K. Nurmagamabetov was appointed Defence Minister, to be replaced by Alibek Kasimov in 1995. A Republican Guard of 25000 men to protect the President and the Parliament was created. Initially, the force-planning by the Kazakhstan Ministry of Defence was based on the criterion that troop numbers should be at least 0.5 per cent of the state's population (i.e. about 83,000). This proved to be unrealistic due to shortage of funds and the inability to enforce conscription consistently. The other serious problem for the Kazakh armed forces is the lack of experienced Kazakh military leadership personnel. About 6,000 Russian troops from the former Soviet 40th Army remained in Kazakhstan to provide military training. According to bilateral agreements with Russia, 500 officers from Kazakhstan are sent to Russian military schools each year.

Nevertheless, Kazakhstan still has to rely on ethnic Slavs for most of its officer corps. The departure of many non-indigenous officers has resulted in a shortage of cadres of more than 50%. In 1993, the International Institute of Strategic Studies' (IISS) Military Balance estimated the strength of the army at 44,000 troops. In 1995 this estimate had declined to 25,000 (with an estimated figure of 40,000 for the armed forces in total). The air force (personnel estimated at 15,000) has 37 fighter ground attack aircraft at its disposal. The social conditions of the army are very poor, soldiers are said to be suffering from lack of food and infectious diseases. Despite officials rhetoric, the army exhibits all the signs of severe neglect. Much of the equipment inherited from the Soviet armed forces is deteriorating due to lack of maintenance. Landlocked Kazakhstan has no navy but intends to form a maritime force. There is a Caspian Sea flotilla, which operates as a joint Russian, Kazakh and Turkmen flotilla under Russian command.[47]

The most important Soviet strategic assets on Kazakh territory were the IBM bases with 104 SS-18, the Semipalatinsk nuclear test site, the Baikonur space launch centre, and the ABM radar site. The disposition of these assets raised many difficulties since on the one hand Kazakhstan could not integrate them into its own military forces, and on the other hand it had an interest in getting the most out of their presence on its soil. Furthermore, President Nazarbayev insisted that all military installations in Kazakhstan were the property of Kazakhstan. The strategic nuclear missiles were shut down as part of the START process and all the nuclear warheads were transferred to Russia as Kazakhstan joined NPT as a non-nuclear power. The Semipalatinsk site was closed. After much political wrangling, the Baikonur space complex was made available to Russia on the basis of 20 year renewable lease.[48]

Kyrgyzstan

The Russian-Kyrgyz military relationship centres around border protection. An inter-governmental agreement, concluded in October 1992, stipulated that in order to ensure its own security, that of the Russian Federation and the collective security of the CIS member-states, Kyrgyzstan delegate the issue of protecting its state border with China to Russian border troops. A subsequent agreement signed in April 1994 established the terms of recruitment and military service of Kyrgyz nationals in the Russian border troops deployed on the territory of Kyrgyzstan. Russia covers 80 per cent and Kyrgyzstan 20 per cent of the expenses of these troops. Russia has also undertaken to help Kyrgyzstan to form its own border troops during the transition period. However, the duration of this transition period has not been specified.

Uzbekistan

"In the unstable world surrounding us we have friends, but there are those as well, who would like to drag Uzbekistan into their sphere of influence. And those forces may use any available methods, including military one. Therefore, we must have a mobile, well-trained and equipped army capable of defending our borders, our independence and sovereignty", said Uzbek President, Islam Karimov.[49] According to Islam Karimov, there could be the following basic perceptions:

- Uzbekistan occupies an extremely favourable geographical location in the Central Asian oil transport, energy and water systems of the region.
- Uzbekistan outnumbers its neighbours and surpasses them in its scientific and technical

potential and other capacities; the Republic has oil, oil products, gas, namely those resources, which are the backbone of any economy. It has every chance to increase its economic potential.

- Uzbekistan occupies a well deserved place in human civilization. It exerts a strong influence on various spiritual and political processes not only in the region, but all over the world.

These concepts, according to the Uzbek policy planners, could throw up good opportunities for Uzbekistan to be at the centre stage of security plan in Central Asia.

At the 48th session of UN General Assembly, Karimov proposed to set up in Tashkent a permanent United Nations seminar on issues of security, well-being and cooperation in Central Asia. In this connection, he claims that "the republic could serve as an outpost in Asia, a bridgehead of co-operation between the OSCE and the United Nations in the provision of regional security and cooperation, preventive diplomacy and conflict resolutions".

As a member of the non-aligned movement, Uzbekistan may have to reconcile its position as a signatory to the collective security agreement signed by her in 1992. But Uzbekistan can argue that the Tashkent Agreement is not providing any basis for formation of a military alignment. Therefore the question of the non-aligned movement refusing her membership would not arise.

Uzbekistan's Military Strength

As has already been stated, Central Asian republics did not have a strong military presence in the Soviet armed forces. Smaller republics like Turkmenistan, Tajikistan, Kyrgyzstan etc. were only nominally represented. Except during the World War II, when there was a great need for manpower, these republics had next to nil representation.

However, it has been reported that the number of soldiers and non-commissioned officers of Uzbek ethnic origin in the Soviet army did not go beyond seven thousand persons. Raising of the proposed army of 30,000 men in addition to Guards depended on availability of funds which, however, are not forthcoming at the moment. All that Russian Federation is capable of providing was military assistance in training, moderate communication equipment and infrastructure. Ultimately with the strengthening of economic conditions the republic will have to raise some units. At the present moment, Uzbekistan is also among those that provided some personnel to the Tajik—Afghan border guards. According to a report the total military hardware available with this republic is about 280 main battle tanks, 780 armoured vehicles, 265 fixed wing aircraft and 24 helicopters.[50]

Turkmenistan

Turkmenistan is a case apart. President Safarmurad Niyazov has not been an easy person to handle either for the Russians or for other leaders of Central Asian republic. The reason is perhaps Turkmenistan's close geographical proximity to Iran. She has a 500 kilometer long border with Iran to her south. There are a large number of Turkmen ethnic people residing in northern Khurasan province of Iran which is contiguous to Turkmenistan. These Turkmens have close affinity with their co-ethnic groups across the international border. Therefore, President Niyazov cannot take any reckless step that might antagonise either his people on the southern border or the Turkmens on the Iranian side of the border. This is a major reason why he distanced himself from any security arrangement because Iran has been sensitive to what she calls invisible hand of the westerners behind these security arrangements.

An international conference on 'Neutrality of Turkmenistan and International Relations in Asia' was held in Turkmen capital Ashkabad in September 1995. The Turkmen President clearly floated the idea of his country's neutrality. He pleaded that he had over 30 per cent of world gas reserves and 12 billion tonnes of oil in the Caspian shelf. He had a population of 5 million and a vast territory. As such the only way for Turkmenistan was to remain neutral, he emphasised. He argued that joining the blocs would jeopardise the concept of neutrality.[51]

Thus instead of becoming a signatory to the Tashkent Agreement or joining the Council of Collective Security of the CIS, Turkmenistan found it convenient to develop bilateral relationship with Russian federation in broad defence matter. It has to be noted that Turkmenistan has common border with Afghanistan also and there have been incidents of border clashes after the declaration of independence by Turkmenistan. There is a proposal of laying the gas pipeline from Daulatabad gas field to Afghanistan via Mazar-e-Sharif and then to Pakistan. This also is a compulsion with Turkmenistan to develop friendly relations with the southern neighbours.

The Russian officers mostly command the 35,000-strong armed force of Turkmenistan, with air forces, air defence forces and rear services at the moment. Defence and National Security Council of Turkmenistan includes a Russian officer who represents the Russian Defence

Ministry. Major General V. M. Zavarzin represents the Russian Defence Ministry at the moment. Obviously, Russian officer will leave one day and the command of units will pass into the hands of the Turkmen officers themselves. Thus Turkmen soldiers are being trained to that purpose.[52]

Bringing Cohesion to Central Asian Defence

It appears that three Central Asian States, namely Kazakhstan, Uzbekistan and Kyrgyzstan have developed a sort of understanding not only in economic field but also in matters of defence. On April 29-30, 1994, Presidents of these three states met in Bishkik where Kyrgyzstan agreed to be a signatory to the creation of a Single Economic Space. The defence alliance, though not in formal manner, remains an understanding among the three. The concept, which has became catalyst to this decision is that economic development is possible only in a state of security and peace.

The decision of forming a Joint Council of Defence Ministers was taken by the above mentioned three states when their Interstate Council met in December 1995 in Jambyl. At that meeting a resolution on a Joint Council of Defence Ministers was also approved. Essential and important matters pertaining to security and defence were the subjects which this Council would be empowered to deal with. The concept of cohesion in defence matters meant joint exercises, mutual supplies, maintenance of arms and equipment or their upgradation and procurement of advanced arms etc.[53] A blue print for coordinating defence efforts was also prepared and circulated so that the terms of reference of the Council of Defence Ministers would be clear and unambiguous.

It had mainly two aspects. The first was individual defence-forming, which meant that the three states were individually free to strengthen and develop their defence capabilities. The second is collective defence-forming. This would be within the framework of CIS.

There has been the 1992 Collective Security Agreement. But what could give teeth to this agreement was a mechanism for its realization. In its absence, the Collective Security does not mean much in terms of real defence strategy and security for Central Asian States. One school of thinkers is disposed to say that there should be a system of Euro-Central Asian Security if one has to be practical and realistic.

In the context of collective security for Central Asia, one cannot lose sight of the role of NATO in the post Soviet period and the dissolution of Warsaw Pact. In a sense Central Asia needs an umbrella security and the member-states of the OSCE and NATO might have a role to play. At the same time, Central Asian States cannot afford to turn away from the situation that is obtaining in regard to the Asian security system. China is another important actor on the scene.

And lastly, the question of integration of Central Asian security system into the global security system has to be taken into consideration. These states have been admitted to the world bodies like the UN. The impact of the decisions of the Security Council or the resolutions of the General Assembly on the defence and security strategies of the Central Asian States will be a reality. This needs to be responded to in a positive manner.

Soviet Hangover

The world has been watching with interest the Russian perception of Central Asia as independent states. Biased observers are wont to carry on the Soviet hangover to the post-Soviet era as well, which is totally unrealistic. There are several strong reasons for that.

There had been the growing feeling in the policy planning circles in Russian that separation of the Central Asian regions and their declaration of independence have been a welcome decision for the Russian Federation. Russia is herself in a state of chaos and confusion with a fragile economy to boot. She is not in a position either to provide a credible defence system to the Central Asian States or to assist them in raising armies and armaments that could be considered sufficiently dependable for providing some semblance of security to Central Asia.

But notwithstanding this phenomenon, Russia cannot announce her total retirement from Central Asian sphere of influence. The loss of Kazakhstan is considered by her a vacuum in security system.[54] The presence of very large Diasporas in Russia and in the Central Asian states of the citizens of respective nativity is an important factor in determining the mutual relations between Russia on the one hand and the Central Asian States on the other.

Russia has some vital interests in different parts of Central Asia. In Kazakhstan, there is sizeable Russian population towards the north. Direct control from Moscow may not be there but economic interests of ethnic Russians will always be a dominant factor in Russian-Kazakh relationship. Russia has already conceded Kazakhstan's sovereignty over the nuclear warheads within Kazakh territory. But the facts of economic system and the presence of ethnic Russians make her impact in the Ural-Western Siberia-Northern Kazakhstan regions an option for her to interact with Almaty.[55]

Russia will essentially take care of the fact that her economic interests in Central Asia are not jeopardized to the extent that she is eliminated from the sphere of influence. As long as the CIS Collective Security Agreement remains, her economic interests are closely linked to it. Two countries in the region, namely Iran and Turkey, could be the possible economic entrepreneurs if Russian economic interests are weakened to a larger extent.[56]

In the context of the growing crescendo of religious extremism in the neighbouring Islamic countries, particularly Afghanistan, Central Asia has serious apprehensions. In the political chemistry of Central Asian States, a definite and conspicuous tilt towards religious extremism, sponsored either by external or internal agencies, is likely to arrest the economic development of the entire Central Asia. These states need foreign exchange, technical know-how, foreign investment, security and expertise and foreign markets etc. Now looking around, it is only Russia which can provide these conditions. Therefore, the position of Russia gets reinforced as a dependable friend. One can see that Russia has now come under direct attack of the religious extremists and this must be a factor with the Central Asians for strengthening their relations with Moscow.[57]

Russia will also take due cognizance of the role of China in Central Asia. It may not be only economic. China has already provided delicate defence technology to Pakistan and missiles to Saudi. She could do it in Central Asia. It appears that Russia has adopted two stances on CA. One is conveying the message to the world that Central Asia falls within the sphere of influence of Moscow and second is that in view of regional threats, Russia has the obligation of ensuring the security of the region.[58]

In terms of Russo-Kazakh relations, it appears some Kazakh observers are trying to exaggerate things. A fear psychosis is being created by quoting the example of maveric Zhirinovsky or Solznetsyn. The inference is that Russia wants to dominate. Such views were also implicit in the statements make by the former Russian Defence Minister, Pavel Grachev, in the spring of 1994, and the then Foreign Minster, A. Kozyrev, in 1995, that the Commonwealth of Independent States is in the Russian sphere of influence, and Russia will protect the Russian population anywhere with the use of force if considered necessary. Although the concept of Russia's national interests has not yet been officially declared, it can be discerned in various documents. The most important is Russia's military doctrine. This continues to be the prevailing feeling.

At the moment, what is of much importance is the new nuclear policy of Russia. There is the option of use of nuclear weapons in specific situations: aggression against a state which is party to the NPT or against an ally of the Russian Federation. The allies include the parties that signed the Collective Security Agreement in May 1992. Kazakhstan, therefore, need not be scared of Russian nuclear option as she is well protected by the treaty. But at the same time, Russia would like to ensure that Kazakhstan is not subjected to blackmailing by outside powers when international agreements in the areas of arms reduction or limitation are sought to be implemented in letter and in spirit.

This point is exemplified by the START I agreement. Russia, the United States, Ukraine, Kazakhstan and Belarus are party to this treaty. If Kazakhstan had not joined the NPT by December 1993, it could have been considered a military threat. Likewise, when the Ukrainian Parliament (the Supreme Rada) declared Ukraine a *de facto* nuclear state, Ukraine became a potential military threat to Russia, giving rise to a whole range of actions to coerce Ukraine into de- nuclearisation.

Russia also considers the violation of the rights of Russian minorities as a potential military threat justifying military intervention. Moscow looks at the socalled Russian speaking population in Kazakhstan (about 50 per cent of the total) as Russian citizens. From 1993 to 1994, Moscow demanded that Kazakhstan recognize the principle of dual citizenship for Russians in Kazakhstan. Hypothetically, Kazakhstan could be considered a threat to Russian national security interests.

It is also clear from Russian military doctrine that the preservations of administrative and military control over strategic nuclear forces, space assets (such as Kazakhstan's space port of Baikonur and any installations) and part of the system of control over strategic nuclear forces is central to Russian national security interests. The document reasserts that nuclear weapons of the former Soviet Union belong to Russia. This puts it automatically in conflict with Ukraine and Kazakhstan.

Russian military doctrine defines the security space of the Russian Federation which is supported by the collective Security Treaty within the framework of the CIS. Russia only used it once in the case of Tajikistan. To fully support the treaty commitments, it requires, in the view of the government of Kazakhstan, expenditures which Russia cannot presently afford.

The adoption of Russian military doctrine and its place in Russian foreign and security policy permits the following conclusions to be drawn:

(a) Russia insisted on the right to follow its own policy in the field of security; that is why it rejected the formation of unified armed forces of the CIS.

(b) Russian estimates that various sources of threats to its national security will emerge. To deal with some of these problems, Russia will sacrifice the sovereignty of its allies.

(c) The solution of the problem of nuclear weapons is closely linked to the solution of Russia's economic problems.

(d) The fundamental paradox of Russian-Kazak relations, as becomes clear in the Russian military doctrine, is that Russia is both the guarantor of Kazakhstan's security and its principal threat. Russia views Kazakhstan as an ally, as part of the sphere of Russian national interest and as a potential military threat.

Peace Under UN Aegis

The presidents of the three countries appealed to the UN Secretary General to send a UN mission for consultations with representatives of their Ministries of Foreign Affairs and Defence, and requested the preparations of the necessary documents in order to join the Agreement on Reserve Forces of the UN. The decision to form a joint peace-keeping battalion operating from the CIS peace-keeping forces reflected concern over the situation in Tajikistan and Afghanistan and probably an understanding on the inefficiency of collective peace-keeping forces in the framework of the CIS. How far would the peace-keeping battalion be effective in keeping peace is a different question. The fact of the matter is that there is the urge among the Central Asian leadership that peace is the most important pre-requisite for economic and social development. The UN role in the promotion of peace has been substantial.

Security Links: Europe and Central Asia

Organisation of Security for Central Europe (OSCE) was theoretically designed to take care of broad security and development questions of Europe. It is true that owing to many differences within the European countries, this Organisation could not get the teeth it needed to be effective. The Organisation has neither the mandate nor funds to retain forces that would be needed for ensuring the security of Europe. As such perhaps Central Asian states cannot expect too much from OSCE. But the fact is that there is a concept that Europe, Euro-Asian Russia, Trans-Caucasia and Central Asia should, by geographical parameters, be taken together while discussing security concerns and perspectives.

Of course the NATO factor has to be taken into account. There is a thinking in some influential circles that NATO could intervene in the case of some trouble-spots but only through the aegis of the UN or the OSCE. But that creates a difficulty. The role of NATO is that this organisation of 16 nations is essentially a military and political alliance with a definite mandate. How far can its role outside the ambit of its terms of reference be acceptable to disputing states remains a debatable proposition.

The question is—what shall happen if Russia, as a member of NATO, approaches it for sanction to peace-keeping in one of the erstwhile federating units of the Soviet Union? Obviously, the impression, which this approach is likely to create, is that Russia wants to further its political and perhaps military influence in the Central Asian region on the basis of her earlier relationship. It is difficult to assume that Russia would misuse her position for any political aggrandizement in Central Asia. She is already committed to the security of Tajik-Afghan border, as an example of the nature of seeking OSCE's support for any intervention in Central Asia.

Admittedly, OSCE is an institution which recognises the law of equality among its members. Central Asian states or the states of the trans-Caucasia or of Euro-Asia are as good members of the institution as any European state. Therefore, security implications are also to be accounted for in terms of equality of status. However, formation of peace-keeping force by the CIS countries is a proposition that is already under consideration. A regional arrangement though necessary and feasible would not necessarily disregard the large arrangement either by the UN or the NATO and OSCE. Their roles are complementary rather than conflicting.

When the former Soviet Union broke up, the Central Asian states became entitled to the membership of OSCE. Security being the essential aim of OSCE, the Central Asian States also got admitted to the concept at its very root. Naturally the Central Asian states decided to strengthen the purpose of this organisation because that went in their own interests. Some important institutions, which form the backbone of a democratic state and society, had to be created and strengthened after the collapse of the Soviet power. Some of these were the legislative and social institutions, human rights and national minority rights institutions and all institutions that helped economic and social reconstruction. In that sense, membership of OSCE proved a boon for the Central Asian States.

The creation of a united Euro-Central Asian space of security and cooperation (if one takes into account the participation of the USA and Canada in the OSCE, then it would be more accurate to talk about a North-

Atlantic and Euro-Central Asian space) does not contradict the efforts of Kazakhstan to convene a conference on Cooperation and Confidence-Building Measures in Asia (CCMA). The latter initiative is derived from the experience of the European security process, namely Defence and Security of Central Europe (DSCE) / Organization of Security for Central Europe (OSCE), and has many similarities with the CSCE/OSCE experience of collaboration with certain Mediterranean countries that are not members of this organisation.

The situation in Central Asia and also in neighbouring regions, which do not participate in the OSCE - China, Afghanistan, Iran, Pakistan and India - is important to strengthen the stability of the OSCE space. In this context, the OSCE should welcome the efforts of Kazakhstan aimed at the convention of CCMA. The OSCE should also accept positively the processes of regional integration in Central Asia, in the CIS as a whole, as well as within the framework of the Economic Cooperation Organisation.

In his study on Central Asian security entitled 'Central Asia: National, Regional and Global Aspects of Security', the Kazakh scholar Oumirserik Kasenov has drawn the following conclusions in regard to realisation of Euro-Central Asian system of security:

(a) It would place the Central Asian region in the field of European processes of security and extend into its territory the common principles of inviolability of frontiers, territorial integrity, etc.

(b) The Central Asian States would enter into a broader security space than the post-Soviet space, which would reduce the domination of

Russia in the Central Asian region and increase opportunities of the OSCE to implement or control peace-keeping operations on its territory.

(c) It would stop disputes about the possible expansion of NATO, diminish friction between Russia and NATO, Russia and the United States Defense Arrangement (USDA), and Russia and the West as a whole in connection with Russia's policy in Eastern Europe and the post-Soviet space. The border between the 'far' and 'near abroad' would be eliminated in favour of a single Euro-Central Asian space of security.

(d) There would emerge a reasonable balance of mutual relations between the OSCE, NATO, and CIS which, as a whole and under the aegis of the UN, might characterise the Euro-Central Asian system of security.

(e) The creation of the Euro-Central Asian system of security would not contradict Kazakhstan's efforts to create a system of security on the Euro-Asian continent.

But the fact of the matter is that these presumptions are not infallible. It has to be remembered that the idea of common principles of inviolability of fronticrs and territorial integrity is as yet a moot question in regard to Central Asian States. For European states, this is an established fact through treaty bodies, tradition and international recognition. But in Central Asia, we still hear the voices that claim the territorial engineering of Soviet days as biased or lop sided or contrary to the historical evidence. This has given rise to the territorial disputes which may be dormant today but are likely to be activated tomorrow.

Secondly, whatever space the Central Asia might find in the new security system, the fact shall remain that Russia will exercise profound influence on the security perceptions of Central Asia. This position is assured by tradition, history and practice. There is no common language other than Russia, which is the binding force among the Central Asian states. The argument that it could stop the dispute about the possible expansion of NATO is not tenable.

As has been observed, the role of NATO has assumed a new dimension. Had not the Soviet Union collapsed, NATO would never have played its role in Federal Republic of Yugoslavia. Under the unipolar power system, NATO is certainly going to step into shoes bigger than its size. There is nothing which can stop world powers from utilising the services of NATO in Central Asia if the exigency of the situation so demands. And finally the idea of emergence of a reasonable balance means very little in the presence of unipolar power structure that is obtained at the moment.

Now one knows that Central Asian States cannot reach the level of military strength as that of their immediate neighbours like Russian Federation and China. They cannot even reach the level of smaller powers like Iran and Turkey. It may, therefore, be possible to think of Central Asian security within the framework of the existing security structures, namely NATO, OSCE etc. This depends mostly on the nature of interests that the western countries and Russia might evince in the progress, sovereignty and development of Central Asia. May be there is a link up between Central Asian and the regional and European security system. There are some hints to that effect. But in that case, the consent of the Russian Federation might become a pre-requisite because Moscow should not consider its encroachment upon her sphere of influence.

Dissolution of Warsaw Pact and 'Partnership for Peace'

The fact is that the dissolution of Warsaw Pact exposed the Central Asian States not only to the external threats but also to internal clashes and tensions. This situation was further exacerbated by the absence of military power in any of the Central Asian States that could be called commensurate with the security requirements of the perspective states.

Western powers lost no time in upgrading and expanding the role of NATO which was hitherto under the shadow of Warsaw Pact. The Central Asian states and especially two bigger states of Kazakhstan and Uzbekistan looked up to NATO as the one filling the vacuum caused by the dissolution of Warsaw Pact. In this context, the following observations of Kazakh President, Nursultan Nazarbayev, are quite interesting :

> The North Atlantic Treaty has a suitable goal for our rapprochement to assist the democratic development of the states of Central and Eastern Europe and the CIS, and to prevent regional conflicts as far as possible.... NATO member-states, for the purpose of cooperation with these states, have committed themselves to proving their accumulated experience and considerable expert potential in defence policy ... Considering all this, we will broaden contacts with NATO, provided their sphere and limits are strictly determined and they are not damaging for military cooperation

within the CIS framework or bilateral military ties.

When both the Soviet Union and its sponsored Warsaw Pact were dissolved, NATO reconsidered its objectives in that changed situation. Thus came into being the North Atlantic Cooperation Council with a new agenda for cooperation. It was given the high-sounding name of 'partnership for peace' (PFP). The new objectives for the NATO have been summed up by the analysts as follows:

- to prevent the emergence under conditions of political uncertainty and economic chaos of new totalitarian regimes and militarized states,
- to prevent the creation within the CIS framework of a new NATO military bloc,
- to prevent the merger of Central Asian States with the Islamic world, especially with the countries where the ideology of orthodox Islam prevails,
- to assist the cooperation of the new states in order to provide regional and global,
- to assist in the creation of the necessary conditions for the democratization of societies in these states.

Soon after the dissolution of Warsaw Pact, NATO, among other measures in Eastern Europe, also paid its attention to Central Asia. Joint programmes have been envisaged and some of these have even been launched. The de-nuclearisation of Kazakhstan has been one of the important facets of the programme for peace to which allusion has already been made. A framework document was signed by the parties concerned. Tajikistan was the only state which could not sign it. The fundamental principle guiding the signing of an agreement for cooperation with NATO is that the organization will assist the states in raising their regular armies, provide them training and infuse it with the democratic norms of a modern state. The role of peace keeping has also been accepted as one of the concerns of these armies.

It has to be remembered that ethnic conflict has been plaguing the Central Asian societies for long. It is because of the long history of nomadic rivalries during the Middle Ages and the scarcity of water and arable land. Even during the Soviet power, there have been ethnic clashes in various parts of Central Asia like those in Ferghana valley or in Tajikistan. NATO has the infrastructure to monitor the occurrence of such conflicts and the wherewithal to impose effective control over them. This has been one of the reasons why the Central Asian States were drawn to the 'Programme for Peace' floated by a NATO.

Cooperation with NATO was begun with a theoretical approach. A number of seminars and conferences concerning the security of Central Asia and the allied matters have been organised and attended. Of course, NATO has not promoted military exercises because such activities are neither required nor are these feasible at this moment. But the problems of security and the principles which should guide the building up of armies and defence structures have been theoretically discussed and debated. Training of officers of Central Asian states has also been an important part of cooperation with NATO. Many officers have visited the military academies in NATO countries and acquainted themselves with the courses of training and related activities.

But this does not mean the NATO shall remain confined only to theoretical exercises and the actual groundwork will be neglected. After all the theory has to be put into use. In this background, we are told that in August 1995, some military units of Central Asian states joined military exercise in USA (in Louisiana) in which the American and Canadian troops had participated. In the following year, NATO prepared more exercises for the combined forces of Central Asia and some of NATO member state forces in North Carolina. Though to our knowledge no military joint exercise has been staged on the soil of Central Asia so far, this cannot be ruled out. Already in 1997, Kazakh forces had drawn a plan with the US armed forces for such an exercise.

Nevertheless such military exercises on Central Asian soil will be looked with some alarm by the Russian Federation. Perhaps some sort of rationalization will have to be made. Conducting large-scale exercise on Central Asian soil is bound to cause irritation to Iran, China and of course Russia. The Central Asian States would not be willing to take that risk. It is, therefore, presumed that NATO and its member states will not be intransigent to push Central Asia into that precarious situation. What Central Asian States like Kazakhstan, Uzbekistan and Kyrgyzstan need to do is to lay emphasis on building national armed forces sufficiently oriented towards promotion of various features of a democratic and progressive society.

In concluding this chapter, it will be said that two main trends have emerged in Central Asia in regard to measures for security and defence. One is the close cooperation of these states as members of CIS with the Collective Security System in which Russia is the main actor. The second trend is that of Central Asian States cooperating with NATO in the post Warsaw Pact. In a sense these two trends appear irreconcilable. As long as Russia remains bogged down in its economic and internal political imbroglio, NATO and its members are likely to make deeper and deeper inroads into Central Asia. But once the downslide in Russia is halted and Russia looks up again on her environs, particularly to the Central Asian region, the free hand with which NATO is handling the prospective security concerns may not be that free.

Another conclusion that is to be drawn is that as long as economic rivalry among the Central Asian States is not exacerbated through internal or external agents, there is less possibility of eruption of ethnic crises in Central Asian States. Surprisingly, contrary to the general opinion, Central Asia has remained peaceful after the implosion of the Soviet Union. This is an indication that once the states are engaged in serious and pervasive economic reconstruction, the angularities like those of ethnic propensities can be ironed out. It is up to these states how they minimise their security threats and requirements and divert their resources to social reconstruction. In more recent times, the nationalist upsurge in Chechnya and Georgia did have an impact on Central Asian States. The anti-Russian elements which have never been fully absent from Central Asia even during the Soviet power, could find impetus for resurgence in case the regimes in these states showed a tendency to go dictatorial. To expect the western type of democracy to prevail in Central Asia would be too idealistic. After all the ground has to be prepared for that system. Nevertheless, given the fact that Central Asia did maintain the semblance of its indigenous culture during the Soviet power, one can guess that the amount of democracy allowed in post-

Soviet era would not be a bad thing. The scope for improvement is always there.

The Bosnian and later on the Kosovar developments in Europe and the reaction of the US and the western world are not without an impact on Central Asia. We have been talking of NATO's role in Europe and in the entire region. Now one knows that NATO performed a practical role in Yugoslavian crisis. One of the reasons why Yugoslavia was subjected to intense NATO bombing for more than two months apart from the repressive policy of Yugoslav President in Kosova, is that Yugoslavia had not agreed to be a member of NATO after the implosion of the Soviet Union. This position of the former socialist republic and pro-Soviet ally was untenable for the NATO members led by the US.

It is also argued that the US and the West decided on NATO strikes on Yugoslavia to send multiple messages to the concerned. One message could be meant for the CIS security preparations in Central Asia.

With the exploration of vast energy resources in Kazakhstan and Turkmenistan in Central Asia, the eyes of the developed countries of the Western world and the US have a different vision of Central Asia. The Gulf oil resources are reported to be of limited capacity. The new fields in Central Asia are reported to be larger and richer than the Gulf fields. For example, Azeri oil field in trans-Caspia is called Caspian Kuwait. The Daulatabad gas field in Turkmenistan attracted major oil and gas cartels of the world and their rivalry ultimately ended up in a shared contract in which major partners, British Petroleum Unocal, and other oil consortia undertook exploration, exploitation and marketing of oil and gas from Central Asia.

It will be mentioned that Turkmenistan had signed an agreement with the Argentinean Company for export of Daulatabad gas to Pakistan via Mazar-e-Sharif and Kabul. However, the American Unocal wrested the contract, and made a deal with the Taliban in Afghanistan for the safety of the pipelines that had to be laid along the route that was charted out. However, this project has not as yet taken off. Nevertheless, the insecurity in Northern Afghanistan and its impact on Central Asia cannot be ignored. Political analysts are presuming that the US and her western allies would be interested in maintaining peace and security in Central Asia so that its energy resources could be tapped for global marketing. This might also mean the presence of western military power in close proximity of Central Asia so that Russia and China do not exercise the monopoly of power in the region. As such the assigned role of NATO in Central Asia has been devised and the modalities adopted are subtle and far-reaching. These have been explained in the foregone paragraphs and need not to be recapitulated.

With a thaw in Iran-American relations, and the moderate policy of President Khatami, there is every possibility that the US would not attempt blocking Iran's path in Central Asia especially in Turkmenistan for exploitation of oil and gas, and in Tajikistan for unfolding of cultural bipartisanship. This could be a stabilising factor and would also help in reducing the dependence of these Central Asian States on Russia. One is aware that there is an enormous network of teaching English language throughout the schools in Central Asian States. It has a number of purposes. Dependence on Russia would be reduced, Central Asia would be exposed to the western developed societies and culture, and she would also find an opening in her technological and scientific research leading to the raising of standard of living of her peoples. A large number of Central Asian students are receiving scholarships from Western universities and the US. This section of youth population is bound to bring about significant changes in the thinking of the people as a whole. A large number of military and air force officers are receiving training in various military academies in the western countries. This is going to change the complexion of the new armed forces that will be raised in Central Asia in times to come.

A word must be added about non-proliferation treaty and the CTBT. Central Asian States remain outside the pale of nuclear club. Kazakhstan has already surrendered the nuclear warheads. No other state in Central Asia has any nuclear weapons. As such, it remains a safe region. But of course, China and Russia are two neighbouring countries with nuclear power at their command. In the wake of these two countries having signed the CTBT and the NPT, there appears little chance of any surprise nuclear attack on Central Asia. The sense of security from nuclear holocaust should induce the local governments to direct their attention towards economic development of their respective peoples with added determination. Though the two neighbouring powers, Russia and China, make a mutual deterrent against the use of the weapons of mass destruction, yet the US would not hesitate to offer nuclear umbrella to the region if and when need arises. This was perhaps one of the subjects that the US and Kazakh negotiators had debated for a long time when the question of withdrawal of nuclear warheads from Kazakhstan was underway. However its details are not known.

Conclusion

1. Internal security of the Central Asian Sates remains in place as long as ethnic, linguistic and other dissensions remain absent or under control.
2. CIS combined security force remains a fragile and temporary proposition as a guarantee of security in the region.
3. Local States in Central Asia are not in a position to raise strong and well-equipped and trained armies to defend themselves against external aggression. It will take them a long time to come up with that option.
4. Central Asian security, therefore, remains subservient to the good relations and goodwill of primarily two major powers in the region, namely Russia and China. But essentially, there has to be an understanding among the three major powers, Russia, China and the US that Central Asia should be left out as inviolable zone.
5. Western powers and the US would not rule out the role of NATO in Central Asia in a situation that hurts the interests of western powers.
6. Existence of vast energy resource in Central Asia (oil in Kazakhstan and Azerbaijan, gas in Turkmenistan, gold and minerals in Uzbekistan and uranium in Tajikistan) could be strong incentives for the big powers to come to an agreement guaranteeing peace in the entire Central Asia, and the economic activity begins on a big scale.

7. Finally, from the circumstances prevailing at the moment, one may assume that right now Central Asia has embarked on an era of development and peace. The question is - can the Central Asian leadership make the best use of this opportunity?

References

1. *The Resurgence of Central Asia, op. cit.,* p. 233.
2. *Strategic Balance*, 1992.
3. *Ibid*
4. Doyle McManus (in Alma Ata) 'Kazakhstan Wants to Keep Nukes', *Dawn*, September, 17, 1991.
5. Reuters, 'Kazakhs To Keep Nuclear Arms'. *Dawn*, January 28, 1992.
6. *Central Asian Significant*, May, 1992.
7. *Resurgence of Central Asia, loc. cit.,* p. 235.
8. Jeffery Smith (in Kieve), Ukraine Ready to Place Warheads Under Supervision'. *Dawn*, June 8, 1993.
9. *US Information Services*, February 4, 1993.
10. 'The Travails of Tajikistan', K.N.Pandita, *The Pioneer*, New Delhi, Decf. 18, 1995.
11. Yuri Vishnesky, Chairman of the Russian State Committee for Safety in the Atomic Industry said that Tajikistan was free to sell uranium ore to whomever it liked. *Trud*, January 9, 1992.
12. Steve Cole (in Alma Ata), 'The Distant Dream on Russia's Rim.' *Dawn*, May 15, 1993.
13. See *Islam and Revolution: Writings and Declarations of Imam Khumeini,* translated and annotated by Hamid Algar, Berkely, 1991, p. 138. See also Martin Kramer, 'Introduction', in M. Kramer (ed.) *Shi'ism Resistance and Revolution*, Boulder, 1987, p. 10.
14. *Ettela'at*, Teheran, August 23, 1991. A few weeks later, he

as Prime Minister stressed that Iran's struggle would continue "until the region and the world are rebuilt upon new foundations". *Teheran Journal*, Oct. 7, 1991.

15. *Keyhan*, Teheran, December 19, 1982.
16. Ramazani, *Revolutionary Iran*, loc. cit., pp. 24 – 51. See also *Current History*, Washington, January 1985, pp. 5 - 6.
17. *Kayahan*, Teheran, October 24, 1983.
18. Statement of Ali Akbar Velayati (*AFP*. January 12, and Deutch Radio (DR), January, 13, 1982, and of Ali Khamenei in *Tehran Times*, Tehran, April 6, 1982.
19. Ramazani, *Iran and the Persian Gulf*, loc. cit. p. 7.
20. Khumeini's message to the Hajj Pilgrims in 1987: Radio Teheran, July 29, and DR July 30, 1987.
21. *Al Zafar*, 19 January, 1985.
22. *Kayhan*. Teheran, February 21, 1985.
23. *Middle East Contemporary Survey*, London, 1978 - 79, pp. 523, 534.
24. *Literaturtante Gazetta*, Moscow, May 13, 1987.
25. S. Agaev. 'The Iranian Revolution', *Nauka l religiia,* II, Paris 1988. p. 26.
26. *Bakinskii rebochii*, Moscow, December 19 and 25, 1981.
27. *Soviet Uzbekistan*, Tashkent, 14 May, 1987.
28. Hans Braeker, 'The Implications of the Islamic Question on Soviet Domestic and Foreign Policy,' *Rerichte des Rundesinnstitus fur astwissenscdhattliche and International Studien*, Bonn, 1983, p. 12.
29. *Azerbayjan genjlari*, November 24, 1987, quoted by Radio Liberty, December 11, 1987.
30. Radio Dushanbe, (in Tajik), May 11, 1988.
31. *Financial Times*, April 14, 1987.
32. *Kommunist Tadzhikistan*, Dushanbe, April 13, 1988, and *Trud*, Moscow, June, 1989.
33. See Patrick Cockburn, 'Dateline USSR: Ethnic Tremors', *Foreign Policy*, Spring, 1989, p. 177.

34. *Izvestia*, November 27, 1988. In Baku, the bands bore the legend 'Karabakh'.

35. Speech of N.N.Ivanushkina at the 13th Plenum of the Uzbek Party Central Committee, *Pravda Vostoku*, May 23, 1989.

36. *Moskovskie Novosti*. Moscow, June 18, 1989.

37. *Trud*, Moscow, June 15, 1989.

38. Anthony Bevins, 'British Plot Aimed to Destabilise Soviets', *Independent*, February 26, 1990.

39. *The Resurgence of Central Asia*, loc. cit., p. 245.

40. Sanobar Shematova, 'Who is Fighting Whom in Tajikistan' in *Russia and the Moslem World*, No. 16, Moscow, 1996.

41. *Ibid*, p. 30.

42. *Moscow News*, No. 6, February 11-18, 1996, p. 11.

43. *Vestnik Voennoy nformatiaii*, Moscow, No./ 11, November 1992, p.7 quoted by Kasenov in *The Himalayan and Central Asian Studies* Journal, New Delhi Vol. 1, No.1, April - June 1997. p. 31 et. seq.

44. *Diplomatichesky Vestnik MID Rossityskoy Federatsii*. Moscow, No. 3, March 1995, p. 35.

45. *Diplomatichesky Vestnik* MID Rossiyskoy Federatsii, No. 3, Moscow, March 1995, p. 35.

46. Robert V. Barylski, Kazakhastan: Military Dimenstaions of State Formation over Central Asia's Civilizational Fault Lines' in Civil - *Military relations in the Soviet and Yugoslav successive States*, Constantine P. Danopouts and Daniel Zirker (eds), Oxford, Westview press, Inc. 1996, pp. 123 - 151. Rechord F. Staar, *The New Military in Russia*, Annapolis, Maryland, USA, Naval Institute Press. 1996, pp. 142 - 144.

47. Barlylski, *Ibid*.

48. Oumirserik Kasenov, 'Central Asia: National, Regional and Gobal Aspects of Security, *loc. cit.*

49. *Pravda Vostoka*, Moscow, Feb. 24, 1995. *Kazakhstani Mirovoe Soobshchestov*. Moscow No. 1, 1995, p. 107.

50. Staar, *op. cit.*, p. 144.

51. *Mezhdunaroanayazhizn*, No. 10, Moscow, 1995.

52. *Ibid.*

53. *Kazakhstanskaya Pravda*, Almaty, December 16, 1995.

54. *International Life*, Moscow, No. 6. 1993, p. 41. See also Akimove A.V. 'Russia and Central Asia: Perspectives of Economic Integration', *Orient*, No. 4, 1994, pp. 120 - 130.

55. *National Doctrine of Russia: Problems and Priorities*, Moscow, 1994, pp. 245 -254.

56. *International Life*, *op. cit.* No. 1, 1993, p. 26.

57. *Asia*, Moscow, No. 1, 1994, p. 2.

58. *Panorama*, Moscow, No. 45, December 1994, p. 5.

59. *Diplomataaichesky vstnik MID Rossiyskoy Federatsii*, Moscow, July 1995, No. 7, p. 44.

CHAPTER V

Central Asia : The New 'Great Game'

A new and important development with bearing on Central Asian security is the situation in Afghanistan that developed after the pull out of the Soviet forces. We shall not deal with the internal situation in Afghanistan in the aftermath of the Soviet pull out, the fratricidal war among various ethnic groups and factions to capture political power. This is a sordid story. In particular, interference by foreign countries in the highly uncertain and unpredictable political scenario in Afghanistan has brought Afghanistan to the brink of disaster. Nearly on half of the country's population is killed, maimed, crippled or has left the country. Civilian institutions and administrative infrastructure is in shambles. A climate of strife has engulfed the country and its people so much so that the world has now begun to write if off.

In these circumstances, there appeared the Taliban militia from the southern town of Kandahar, which did not enjoy much strategic importance for Afghanistan in the past. Nevertheless, as the nerve centre of the Taliban power, Kandahar assumed importance and the attention of world powers was drawn to it. As the Taliban moved northwards, capturing town after town and garrison after garrison, it finally took Kabul by storm and ousted the opponents who moved northward in the Punjsheer Valley that touches on the southern borders of Tajikistan republic. The veteran commander of the resistance force, Ahmad Shah Masud, had been the defence minister in the previous government. But when the Taliban began including ethnic element in the politics of Afghanistan — and perhaps for the first time with serious implications — Ahmad Shah rallied the Tajik ethnic population of the Panjsheer Valley and the northern regions by his side. He set up the resistance government with Burhanuddin Rabbani as its President.

Three countries, Saudi Arabia, Pakistan and the Emirates have formally recognised the Taliban regime of Kabul. But the international community continues to confer on Burhanuddin Rabbani's regime the legitimacy of a valid government. It continues to occupy the seat at the United Nations despite protests by the Taliban regime in Kabul. The fighting between the two groups rages in its furry. Many efforts by some friendly countries and also by the United Nations' agency to bring about reconciliation between the warring groups have not yielded results. As such the suffering and privation of the common people of Afghanistan continues unabated. Since international law and international obligations in regard to the violation of human rights do not guide the warlords, the rights of women and children have been brutalised. Hundreds of thousands of refugees have moved out of Afghanistan and taken the route either to Pakistan or to Iran. Many have fled to the neighbouring Tajikistan. Presence of hundreds of thousands of poverty-stricken refugees has made the situation difficult for the host countries especially when they have their own problem. In particular, Tajikistan, the southern Central Asian State, that has gone thourgh many traumatic situations since the independence in 1991, is virtually unable to provide adequate support and relief to the refugees temporarily encamping on her border close to that of Afghanistan.

The presence of Afghan refugees in Tajikistan in our immediate concern because we shall be trying to trace the impact of Afghan internal situation to Tajikistan and by virtue of its wider ramifications, on the entire Central Asian region in term of security and peace.

The New Great Game

Presence of enormous mineral wealth in Central Asia and the strategic importance of the region have made the whole of Central Asia vulnerable to new political and economic inroads by world powers, particularly the US and some European countries. The impact of hydrocarbon reserves has whetted the appetite of the big powers, and they are trying to induct the element of security concerns to the existing scenario. The scramble for oil and influence by the big powers in the Caspian has been likened to the Middle East in the 1920s. But Central Asia today is an even larger complex guagmire of competing interest. Big power such as Russia, China and the USA; the neighbours Iran, Pakistan, Afghanistan and Turkey; the Central Asian state themselves and the most powerful players of all, the oil companies, compete in what is called 'The New Great Game.

On 12 December 1991, the Central Asian leaders had gathered at Ashkabad in Turkmenistan to discuss the dismemberment of the Soviet Union. They were all reluctant nationalists, full of fear at the prospect of losing the security and support of the Soviet state system and the prospects of facing the outside world on their own. Within a few months, as their economies crumbled, the importance of their oil resources and the need for pipelines became evident. They began to hold talks with Western oil companies, on the back of ongoing negotiations between Kazakhstan and the US company Chevron. But with Afghanistan distintegrating into a civil war, its repercussions were to rebound on Central Asia and the issue of pipelines was to determine the future geo-politics of the region.

"Turkestan, Afghanistan, Transcaspia, Persia — to many these words breathe only a sense of utter remoteness, or a memory of strange vicissitudes and to moribund romance. To me, I confess they are pieces on a chessboard upon which is being played out a game for the domination of the world," wrote Lord Curzon, before he became the Viceroy of India in 1998.

The centre of gravity for both powers was Afghanistan. The British feared that a Russian thrust on Heart from the Turken region could threaten British Maluchistan, while Moscow fold could turn Kabul's rulers against the British. The Russians feared that the Brisitsh would undermine them in Central Asia by supporting revolts by the Muslims tribes and the rulers of empires indulged in massive railway projects. The Russians built railway line across Central Asia to their borders with Afghanistan, Persia and China, while the British built railway line across India to their border with Afghanistan.

Today's Great Game is also between expanding the and contracting empires. As a weakened and bankrupt Russia attempt to keep a grip on what it still views as its frontiers in Central Asia and control the flow of Caspian oil through pipelines that traverse Russia. The USA is thrusting itself into the region on the back of proposed oil pipeline, which would by pass Russia, Iran, Turkey and Pakistan area. These countries may build their own communication links with the region and would want to prefer routes of choice for future pipelines heading east, west or south. China wants to secure stability for its restive Xinijiang region populated by the same Muslim ethnic groups that inhabit Central Asia, secure the necessary energy to fuel its rapid economic growth and expands political influence in a critical border region. The Central Asian state have their own rivalries, preferences and strategic imperatives. Looming above this is the fierce competition between America, European and Asian oil companies.

Afghanistan Central Asian Links

Afghanistan had held Central Asia in a tight embrace for centuries. The territory comprising modern day Tajikistan, Southern Uzbekistan and northern Afghanistan was on contiguous region for centuries, ruled intermittently by Amirs or kings in Bukhara or Kabul. The Amir of Bukhara depended on Afghan mercenaries for his army. Persecuted tribal chiefs, bandits and mullahs sought sanctuary in each other's territories. Thus Tajikistan's decision in 1997 to hand over the Kulyab airbase in southern Tajikistan to Ahmad Shah Mas'ud so that he could receive military supplies from Iran and Russia was but a continuation of these past linkages 3. Afghanistan's continuality with Central Asia came to an end after the 1917 Russian Revolution, when the Soviet Union sealed its borders with its southern Muslim neighbours. The reopening of these borders in 1991 heralded the start of the new Great Game.

Afghanistan today border Turkmenistan, Tajikistan and Uzbekistan but only Turkmenistan has large energy resources. Along the Pamir Mountains, Tajikistan's five million people share a rugged 640-mile border with Afghanistan, which is divided by the Amy Darya river. A quarter of Afghanistan's population is Tajik. More

Tajiks are scattered throughout the other CARs and another 200,000 live in China's Xinjiang province. The only major ethnic Persian tribes who inhabited Central Asian between 1500 and 1000 BC but were later pushed to the peripheries by a series to Turkic invasions from Mongolia.

A few months after the 1917 Revolution, Muslim guerrilla groups sprang up across Central Asia to resist the Bolsheviks. Determined to undermine Soviet power, the British helped the basmachis in 1919, by paying Kabul's rulers to send camel caravans of arms and ammunition to the basmucis. Thousands of Tajik Basmachis took refuge in northern Afghanistan as their struggle continued until 1929, when the Bolsheviks finally crushed them. In another replay in 1980s, the USA encouraged the Afghan Mujahideen to cross into Central Asia and attack Soviet army posts. And in reply soviet troops in Afghanistan frequently called the Mujahideen 'Basmachis'

The Tajik factor

Ultimately the neo-communist government and the Islamicist opposition tin Tajikistan agreed to an UN-brokered peace settlement, but neither side had been able to promote a national identity for the fragmented Tajik clans. These internal cleavages and the fact that it lacked an indigenous intelligentsia to elaborate nationalism linking the people to the land and each other left the country vulnerable to influences from Afghanistan.

Tajikistan remained an underdeveloped, poverty-stricken Republic on the Soviet Union's periphery. Its budged depended on subsidies from Moscow. After 1991, tensions between the Uzbeka and the Tajika and intra-

.... rivalries within the Tajiks erupted. The resulting civil war (1992-1997) between the neo-communist government and an array of Islamicist forces northern Afghanistan, while Tajik government forces were backed by Russian troops. President Boris Yeltsin declrare in 1993 that the Tajik-Afghan border was 'in effect Russia' border' and the 25,000 Russian troops stationed there would be defending Russia. 4

Both sides, the Islamicists and non-communist in Tajikistan, locked as they were in a civil war, eventually co-operated with Mus'ud, who to many Tajiks became a symbol of Tajik nationalism as he battled against the Taliban. The Taliban added to Masud's image by accusing him of trying to divide Afghanistan and create a "Greater Tajikistan' by joining Afghanistan's Badkhshan province with Tajikistan. For Tajikistan the Taliban represented an Islamic fundamentalist at odds with the moderate, Sufi Spiritualism of Central Asia While Pashtun expansionims was at direct odd with Tajik aspirations.

Uzbek factor

Uzekistan is the largest CAR with a population of 22 million. And with some six million Uzbeks living in the other CARs — forming substantial minorities in three of them (Tajikistan, Turkmenistan and Kazakhstan) - Uzbek President Islam Karimov has ethnic allies to pursue his agenda of dominating the region. Some two million Uzbeks live in northern Afghanistan, the result of migrations before and during the Basmachi rebellion. Another 25,000 Uzbeks live in China's Xinjiang province.

Before Soviet troops withdrew from Afghanistan, Moscow and Tashkent were cultivating Afghan Uzbeks to create a secular Uzbek-controlled 'cordon sanitaire' in northern Afghanistan that would resist any Mujahideen takeover. For nearly a decade that policy was successful. General Rashid Dostum controlled six provinces and with military aid from Moscow and Tashkent, held off the Mujahidden and later the Taliban. Karimov meanwhile led the attempt to forge an anti-Taliban alliance amongst the CARs and Russia after 1994. However, with the fall of Mazar-e-Sharif in 1998, Karimov's policy collapsed and the Taliban were now Uzbekistan's immediate neighbours. Since then Uzbekistan's influence in Afghanistan has waned considerably as Karimov was unwilling to back Mas'ud, a Tajik.

Karimov run a tightly controlled, authoritarian police state and cities the civil wars in Afghanistan and Tajkisitan as justification for repression at home. The most significant opposition to Karmove has come from underground radical Islamic groups, some of them Wahhabis, entrenched in the Ferghana valley. Many of these Uzebk militants studies secretly in Saudi Arabia and Pakistan or trained in Afghan Muhahideen camps in the 1980s. Subsequently they developed links with the Taliban.

Uzbekistan is a major player in the new Great Game. It produces sufficient oil and gas for domestic consumption and will soon be an exporter. Initially the oil companies who scrambled to sign contracts with Tashkent's neighbours ignored Uzbekistan. Karimov was both jealous and envious of their success in attracting foreign investment, even as he refused to loosen state controls on the economy to attract Western investors. As Tashkent becomes an energy exporter it will have a vested interest in trying to influence routes for pipelines that benefit Uzbekistan, but it will also act a spoiler in its determination not to see its neighbours prosper and thus become more influential in the region.

Turkmen factor

Turkmenistan's dilemma was that its gas and oil pipeline route through Iran was not acceptable to the USA because of strained relations between the two countries. By 1992, Ukraine, Armenia and then even Russia refused to pay their bills for Turkmen gas imports. Moscow had a stranglehold as all Turkmen gas was pumped through the vast former Soviet pipeline network that was now owned by Russia. President Safarmurad Niyazov of Turkmenistan shut down gas supplies to his neighbours after Turkmenistan accumulated over US $1 billion in unpaid bills and Turkmen gas production slipped to 0.73 tied in 1994, less than a quarter of what it was five years earlier.

Niyazov tried to woo the USA while seeking Teheran's help in developing road and rail links. In December 1997, the Iranians completed construction of a 119 mile long gas pipeline between the Korpedzhe gas field in Western Turkmenistan to Kord-Kuy in Northeastern Iran. This is still the only new pipeline built between Central Asia and the outside world after nearly a decade of trying.

Turkmenistan has the largest gas field in Daulatabad. As Niyazov saw his economy crumble he sought alternative export routes. On the drawn boards in 1994, were plans for a 5,000-mile long oil and gas pipeline castwards to China that would cost over US 20 billion. But the project is still only in the feasibility stage. Also in 1994, Bridas, the Argentinean oil company, which had concessions in Turkmenistan, proposed building a gas pipeline that would cross Afghaistan and deliver gas to Pakistan and India. The US company Unocal with support from Washington proposed a similar pipeline in 1995. The battle between the two companies to build this pipeline sucked in Taliban and the other Afghan warlords. Thus Afghanistan became the fulcrum of the first battle of the new Great Game.

Weak and impoverished and with no military force to defend its long borders with Iran, Afghanistan ad its rival Uzbekistan, Turkmenistan opted for a foreign policy of neutrality. This gave the Rurkmens the justification to keep their distance from Russia and avoid being sucked into the economic and military pacts that arose out of the break up of the Soviet Union. Neutrality also allowed Ashkhabad to avoid taking sides in the Afghan conflict, which angered Moscow and Tashkent as Turkmenistan refused to join the anti-Taiban alliance. Ashkhabad had provided the communist regime in Afghanistan with diesel fuel until Kabul fell in 1992. It proceeded to do the same for Ismael Khan who controlled heart until 1995 and later the Taliban. While the Turken Consulate in Heart maintained good relations with the Taliba, its Consulate in Mazar-e-Sharif did the same with the anti-Taliban alliance. Turkenistan was the only CAR that wooed the Taliban rather than confronted them.

Turkey

Until 1991, Pan-Turkism — the idea of a Turkic homeland stretching from the Mediterranean to China — was a romantic dream espoused by a few Turkish scholars and barely figured in Turkey's foreign policy agenda. Suddely, after 1991, Pan-Turkism became an achievable reality and an integral part of Turkey's foreign policy. The CAR began seeing Turkey as a model for their economic development. Muslim but secular — while Turkey desired to expand its influence in the region and become a major player on the world stage.

Turkey has become a major player in the new Great Game. Its need for energy and desire to expand its influence prompted successive Turkish governments to push for becoming the principal; route for Central Asian energy exports. In the summer of 1997, the USA and Turkey jointly sponsored the idea of a 'transportation corridor' for a main oil pipeline from Baku in Azerbaijan through Georgia and the Caucasus to Turkey's Ceyhan port on the Mediterranean. Kazakhstan and Turkmenistan would be encouraged to feed their oil into this pipeline. This, the USA argued, would give the expansive and lengthy Baku-Ceyhan route the necessary oil volumes to make the project financially viable.

The Azerbaijan International Operating Company, made up of nearly a dozen of the world's oil companies and which dominated Azerbaijan's oil development, was averse to the Baku-Ceyhan route because it was too expensive, to long and would cross Turkey's volatile Kurdish region. By 1998, it was clear that US plans to develop the Afghanistan route would be delayed and so the Baku-Ceyhan corridor became the main plank of Washington's policy towards the Caspian region.

Turkey had backed the Afghan Mujahideen in the 1980s, but its role remained limited. However, as it developed a Pan-Turkic foreign policy, Ankara began to actively support the Turkic minorities in Afghanistan such as the Uzbeks. Ankara provided financial support to General Dostum and twice gave him a home in exile. Turkey became vehemently opposed to the Taliba, which had created a new tension with its close ally Pakistan. Moreover, the Taliban threat had also pushed Turkey in a greater understanding with its regional rival Iran.

Israel

Turkey also played a role in turning around Israel's policy in Afghanistan. Turkey and Israel had developed close military and strategic ties after the 1993 Oslo

Accords. The Israelis and more significantly some Jewish lobbies in the USA were not initially critical of the Taliban. In line with the US State Department, Israel saw the Taliban as an anti-Iranian force, which could be used to undermine Iranian influence in Afghanistan and Central Asia. Moreover the Unocal pipeline across Afghanistan would impede Iran from developing its own pipeline from Central Asia.

Israel's intelligence agency Mossad developed a dialogue with the Taliban through Taliban liaison offices in the USA and with the oil companies. Pakistan's ISI supported this dialogue. Even though Pakistan did not recognize Israel, he ISA had developed links through the CIA wiıh Mossad during the Afghan jihad. With initial support from Turkey, Israel also developed close diplomatic and economic links with Turkenistan, Uzbekistan and Kazakhstan. Israeli companies invested in agriculture the oil industry and communications.

But as the US policy towards the Taliban shifted so did Israel's as the Taliban gave refuge to Bin Laden and encouraged the drug trade. Turkey convinced Israel that the Taliban were a security threat to the region and could export Islamic fundamentalism to Central Asia. As the Unocal project evaporated and Israel realised the aversion its Central Asian allies and Turkey had towards the Taliban, Mossad opened contact with the anti-Taliban alliance. Israel now had an interest in seeing that the Taliban did not take control of the whole of Afghanistan, even though it remained suspicious of Ahmad shah Mas'ud's support from Iran. Both the Taliban and the Northern Alliance were to accuse each other of receiving Israeli support.

Iran

With oil prices crashing in 1999, Iran remained the

wildcard in the new Great Game Iran sits on the second largest gas reserves in the world and has over 93 bb of proven oil reserves with current oil production at 3.6 million/bd. As pipeline projects waned due to low oil prices, Iran stepped in to urge the CARs to expert their oil through a direct north-south pipeline to the Gulf va Iran. Tis could be built at a fraction of the cost of new pipelines across Turkey, because Iran already had an extensive pipeline network ad only needed to add pipeline spurs to connect Iran with Azerbaijan. "The Iranian route for Central Asian oil is the safest, most economic and easiset. The total cost for Iran would be US $300,000. How does that compare with US 3 billion for a pipeline through Turkey," said Ali Majdi, Iran,'s Deputy Minister of Oil. Moreover, ran was also in competition with Turkmenistan to build a gas export pipeline to India and Pakistan — a much more attractive route because it would avoid Afghanistan.

Since 1998, crude from Kazakhstan and Turkmenistan had been transported across the Caspian Sea to Iran's Caspian port of neka, where it is refined and consumed in Iran. In exchange, Iran allowed companies to lift oil from Iranian ports on the gulf. With pipeline projects indefinitely delayed, this appealed to the oil companies who, despite US pressures not to do so, began to negotiate further swaps with Iran. Two US companies, Chevron and Mobile who have oil concessions in Kazakhstan and Turkmenistan applied to the Clinton administration in May 1998 for a licence to carry out swaps with Iran. This was a move that created a major policy headache for Washington and would become a test case for the future of US sanctions against Iran.

Ultimately, the security needed to build pipeline from Central Asia to South Asia rested on ending the

Afghan civil war. "The CARs have two problems with Afghanistan. One is fear and the other is opportunity," the UN mediator for Afghanistan, Lakhdar Brahimi told the correspondent of Daily Telegraph. "Fear is the realization by these new and still fragile countries that the Afghan conflict cannot be contained for ever within its borders. Either it is resolved or it will spill over into the CARs. They want to avoid adventures of any kind from Kabul, be it Islamic fundamentalism, terrorism or drugs. The opportunity is that as landlocked countries that want to break their dependence on Russia, they are looking south for oil and gas pipeline and communication routes. They want a government in Kabul, which is responsible and is a good neighbour. They want to open their borders not close them," Brahimi said.

Despite declining oil prices and Russia's desperate economic plight, the battle of wills between the USA and Russia will dominate future pipeline competition. Russia remains adamant in keeping the USA out of its Central Asian backyard. "We cannot help seeing the uproar stirred up in some Western countries over the energy over the energy resources of the Caspian. Some seek to exclude Russia from the game and undermine its interests. The so-called pipeline war in the region is part of the game," said President Boris Yeltsin in 1998.

US View of Taliban

After the end of the Cold War, Washington's policy to the Afghanistan-Pakistan-Iran-Central Asia region was stymied by the lack of a strategic framework. The USA dealt with issues as they came up, in a haphazard, piecemeal fashion, rather than applying a coherent, strategic, vision to the region. There are several district phases of US policy towards the Taliban, which were driven by domestic American politics or attempted quick-fix solutions rather than a strategic policy.

Between 1994 and 1996, the USA supported the Taliban politically through its allies Pakistan and Saudi Arabia, essentially because Washington viewed the Taliban as anti-Iranian, anti-Shia and pro-Western. The USA conveniently ignored the Taliban's own Islamic fundamentalist agenda, its suppression of women and the consternation they created to Central Asia largely because Washington was not interested in the larger picture. Between 1995 and 1997, the US support was even more driven because of its backing for the Unocal project — even though at the time the US had no strategic plan towards accessing Central Asian energy and thought that pipelines could be built without resolutions to regional civil wars.

The US policy turnaround from late 1997 to the day was first driven exclusively by the effective campaign of American feminists against the Taliban. As always with the Clinton agenda, domestic political concerns outweighed foreign policy-making and the wishes of allies. Clinton only woke up to the Afghanistan problem when American women knocked on his door. President and Mrs. Clinton had relied heavily on the American female vote in the 1996 elections and on female support during the Monica Lewinsky saga. They could not afford to annoy liberal American women.

In 1998 and 1999, the Taliban's support for Bin Laden, their refusal to endorse the Unocal project or compromise with their opponents and the new moderate government in Iran provided additional reasons for the USA to get tough with the Taliban. But it will be remembered that there was not a word of US criticism after the Taliban captured Heart in 1995 and threw out thousands of girls from schools. In fact the USA, along with Pakistan's ISI, considered Heart's fall as a help to Unocal and tightening the noose around Iran. Washington's aim of using the Taliban to blockade Iran was equally shortsighted, because it was to pitch Iran against Pakistan, Sunni against Shia and Pashtun against non-Pashtun. "Whatever the merits of the isolating policy towards Iran in the fight against terrorism, they incapacitated the US in Afghanistan," wrote Barnett Rubin. Iran, already paranoid about CIA plots to undermine it, went into overdrive to demonstrate CIA support for the Taliban while stepping up its own arming of the anti-Taliban alliance "US policy is forcing us to join Russia and anti-Taliban alliance against Pakistan, Saudi Arabia and the Taliban," said an Iranian diplomat.

Some US diplomats, concerned with the lack of direction in Washington on Afghanistan, have admitted that there was no coherent US policy, except to go along with what Pakistan and Saudi Arabia wanted. In a confidential 196 State Department memo written just before the Taliban captured Kabul, analysts wrote that, if the Taliban expanded, Russia, India and Iran would support the anti-Taliban alliance and the war would continue; that the USA would be torn between supporting its old ally Pakistan and trying to prevent antagonising India and Russia with whom the USA was trying to improve relations. In such a situation, the State Department surmised, the USA could not hope to have a coherent policy towards Afghanistan.

There was another problem. Few in Washington were interested in Afghanistan. Robin Raphel, the US Assistant Secretary of State for South Asia and the key policy maker for Washington's Afghan policy at the time, privately admitted that there was little interest in here initiatives on Afghanistan higher up the chain of command in Washington. Secretary of State Warren Christopher never mentioned Afghanistan once during his entire tenure. Raphel's attempts to float the idea of an international arms embargo on Afghanistan through the UN Security Council drew little support from the White House. In May 1996 she managed to push through a debate on Afghanistan in the UN Security Council — the first in six years. And in June, Senator Harik Brown, with support from Raphel, held Senate Hearings on Afghanistan and conducted a three-day conference in Washington between leaders of the Afghan factions and the US legislators, which Unocal helped fund.

Raphel recognized the dangers emanating from Afghanistan. In May 1996 she told the US Senate, "Afghanistan has become a conduit for drugs, crime and terrorism that can undermine Pakistan, the neighbouring Central Asian states and have an impact beyond Europe and Russia." She said extremist training camps in Afghanistan were exporting terrorism.

When the Taliban captured Kabul in September 1996, the CIA again encouraged by ISI analysis, considered that a Taliban conquest of the country was now possible and that the Unocal project could reach fruition. The USA was silent on the Taliban's repression of Kabul's women and the dramatic escalation in fighting and in November, Raphel urged all states to engage the Taliban and not isolate them. "The Taliban control more than two-thirds of the country, they are Afghan, they are indigenous, they have demonstrated staying power. The real source of their success has been the willingness of many Afghans, particularly Pashtuns, to tacitly trade unending fighting and chaos for a measure of peace and security, even with severe social restrictions," said Raphel. It is not in the interests of Afghanistan or any of us here that the Taliban be isolated", she added.

The Unocal and US wanted to believed that the Taliban would win and went along with Pakistan's analysis that they would. The most naive US policy-makers hoped that the Taliban would emulate US-Saudi Arabia relations in the 1920s. "The Taliban will probably develop like the Saudis did. There will be Aramco, pipelines, an emir, no parliament and lots of Sharia law. We can live with that", said one US diplomat. Given their suspicious, it was not unexpected that the anti-Taliban alliance, Iran and Russia, should view the Unocal project as an arm of US-CIA foreign policy and as the key to US support for the Taliban. Unocal's links with the US government became a subject of massive speculation. US commentator Richard Mackenizie wrote that the CIA and the ISI. 17 were regularly bribing Unocal.

Unocal did not say whether it received any support from the State Department or not. However it denied links with the CIA. The US government was aware of Unocal's political neutrality. However its failure was that it never developed a relationship with the Afghan factions, which were independent of the US and Pakistan governments.

There was another a bigger problem. Until July 1997 when Strobe Talbot made his speech in Washington, the USDA had no strategic plan for accessing Central Asia's energy. US oil companies were faced with what they could not do, rather than what they could do since they were forbidden to build a policy of a 'transport corridor' from the Caspian to Turkey (avoiding Russia and Iran). However, the oil companies were reluctant to oblige given the costs and the turbulence in the region. The essential issue, which the USA declined at tackle, was peace-making in the region. Until there was an end to the civil wars in Central Asia and the Caspian (Afghanistan, Tajikistan, Georgia, Chechnya, Nagorno-Karabakh, the

Kurdish issue) and there was a broad consensus with Iran and Russia, pipelines would neither be safe to build nor commercially feasible, as every step of the way Iran and Russia would block or even sabotage them.

It was in the interests of Iran and Russia to keep the region unstable by arming the anti Taliban alliance, so that US pipeline plans could never succeed. Even today the USA is muddled on the critical question of whether it wants to save Central Asia" depressed economist by letting them export energy any way they like or to keep Iran and Russia under blockade as far as pipelines are concerned.

The USA and Unocal were essentially faced with a simple question in Afghanistan. Was it preferable to rely on Pakistan and Saudi Arabia to deliver the Taliban and obtain a temporary Afghan consensus in the old-fashioned way by re-conquering the country? Or was it preferably for the US to engage in peacemaking and bring the Afghan ethnic groups and factions together to form a broad-based policy was to support a widely based, multi-ethnic government in Kabul, the USA for a time believed in the Taliban and when it ceased to do so, it was not willing to rein in Pakistan and Saudi Arabia.

Although there was no CIA budget for providing arms and ammunition to the Taliban and Unocal did not channel military support to the Taliban, the USA did support the Taliban through its traditional allies Pakistan and Saudi Arabia, accepting their provision of arms and funding to the Taliban. "The US acquiesced in supporting the Taliban because of our links to the Pakistan and Saudi governments who backed them. But we no longer do so and we have told them categorically that we need a settlement," the high ranking US diplomat dealing with Afghanistan said in 1998.

Washington's change of heart over the Taliban in late 1997 also arose because of the deteriorating political and economic crisis in Pakistan. US officials began to voice fears that the drugs, terrorism and Islamic fundamentalist threat, which the Taliban posed, could overwhelm its old and now decidedly fragile ally Pakistan. The USA warned Pakistan of the increasing dangers it faced, but became frustrated with the ISI's refusal to pressures the Taliban to be more flexible on the political and gender fronts.

Secretary of State Madeleine Albright made the first public expression of the US change when she visited Islamabad in November 1997. On the steps of Pakistan's Foreign Office she called the Taliban 'despicable' for their gender policies. Inside, she warned Pakistani officials that Pakistan was becoming isolated in Central Asia — which weakened US leverage in the region. But the Sharif regime remained at odds with itself, wanting to became an energy conduit for Central Asia, wanting peace in Afghanistan but insisting this would best be achieved by a Taliban victory. Pakistan couldn't have a Taliban victory, access to Central Asia, friendship with Iran and an end to Bin Laden-style terrorism, all at the same time. It was a self-defeating, deluded and contradictory policy, which Pakistan refused even to acknowledge.

Albright's private criticism of Pakistan's policies and public criticism of the Taliban was followed up by the visit of the US Ambassador to the UN, Bill Richardson, to Islamabad and Kabul in April 1998. But with Pakistan exerting no real pressure on the Taliban, except advising them to give Richardson full protocol, the trip turned into little more than public relations exercise. Richardson's agreements with the Taliban were rescinded hours later by Mulla Omar. The only positive spin from the trip was that it convinced Iran that the USA now saw Teheran as dialogue partner in future Afghan peace talks, thereby reducing US Iranian tensions over Afghanistan.

It appeared that the US was not willing to get deeply involved in Afghan crisis. The Pakistanis realised this weakness and tried to negate US pressure. Foreign Minister Gowhar Ayub blasted the Americans just before Richardson arrived." The Americans are thinking of putting puppets there (in Kabul). These are people who hover around in Pakistan from one cocktail party to the other, they do not cut much ice because they have no support in Afghanistan", Ayub said on a visit on Tokyo."

US tension with Pakistan increased substantially after Bin Laden's attacks against US Embassies in Africa in August 1998. The facet that the ISI had helped introduce Bin Laden to the Taliban in 1996 and had maintained contacts with him, but now declined to help the Americans catch him, created major difficulties in the relationship. The American tone became much harsher, "There appears to be a pervasive and dangerous interplay between the politics of Pakistan and the turmoil inside Afghanistan. With the emergence of the Taliban there is growing reason to fear that militant extremism, obscurantism and sectariantism will infect surrounding countries. None of those countries has more to lose than Pakistan if "Talibanisation' were to spread further", said US Deputy Secretary of State Strobe Talbott in January 1999.

Conclusion

Afghanistan's role has become crucial to the security scenario of Central Asia. At present, all attention is focussed on what happens in Afghanistan. Since Iran and Russia are supporting the Northern Alliance led by Nurhanuddin Rabbani, Tajikistan, the contiguous Central Asian Republic cannot escape the vital role it has to play in blocking the northward march of the Afghan jihadis. How long will Ahmad Shah Mas'ud withstand the onslaught of the Taliban is a moot question. Having ousted Ahmad Shah from his stronghold in the Panjsheer valley, will the Taliban rest content with their complete away over Afghan territory or will they carry the Islamic revolution onward into Tajikistan, remains to be seen.

As already hinted, there is growing alarm and awareness of the fundamentalist threats to the neighbouring states in Central Asia. Working Groups against Terrorism have been formed between the US and Russia and the US and India. These are meeting at intervals to assess the changing situation in the region with impact on Central Asia. The spheres of the countries that are in close proximity to the impending threat are trying to co-ordinate their resistance efforts. In the process the latest to be mentioned is what is called the Shanghai Cooperation Organisation formed on 14 June 2001 in Shanghai in China. The presidents of China, Kazakhstan, Kyrgyzstan, Uzbekistan and Tajikistan and the Prime Minister of Russia met and signed the agreement for the creation of the organistion. It says of "There Evils' namely terrorism, separatism and extremism threatening the entire region and resolves to meet the challenge concertedly. Though there is no mention of any country or group (Pakistan or Afghanistan or Taliban) in formal statements, yet the finger does very subtly point towards these countries and their religious extremist organisations. Tajikistan and Uzbekistan are more worried because Tajikistan has a border that meets with Afghanistan and the fear that trans-border infiltration of armed men cannot be fully checked. In Uzbekistan the Sunni-Wahhabi stronghold of Ferghana valley has been the source of fundamentalist upsurge.

The presence of hydrocarbon energy sources in Central Asia has given a new dimension to her security concerns. The US and other European powers are interested in Central Asia. Again, Central Asia is the buffer between China and the West. Thus we find that at present Central Asian region is getting deeply involved in global politics and geopolitical strategies. For the time being, big powers, including China, are playing a pro-Central Asian card more because of their own security concerns. But once the threat of terrorists, separatists and extremists dogging some vulnerable segments in the region is over or allayed, there is every possibility that the classical 'Great Game' in Central Asia may reappear with new formulations and contours. Whatever the case, hydrocarbon sources in the Central Asian region including the Caspian Shelf are going to play the most crucial role in near future.

checked. In Uzbekistan the Soviet-Wahhabi stronghold of Ferghana Valley has been the source of fundamentalist pressure.

The presence of enormous energy resources in Central Asia has given a new dimension to her security concerns. The US and other European powers are interested in Central Asia. Again, Central Asia is the buffer between China and the West. Thus we find that at present Central Asian region is getting deeply involved in global politics and geopolitical strategies. For the time being, big powers, including China, are playing a predominant Asian card more because of their regional security concerns. But once the threat of terrorism, particularly Islamic terrorism dogging some vulnerable segments in the region is downplayed, there is every possibility that the classical 'Great Game' in Central Asia may reappear with new formulations and contours. Whatever the case, hydrocarbon sources in the Central Asian region including the Caspian Shelf are going to play the most crucial role in near future.

Appendix

Data and Chronologies

Uzbekistan

Data

Population: 22 million (Uzbeks 71per cent, Russians 10.8 per cent, Tajiks 4 per cent and Tatars 4.2 per cent).

Total labour force: 8.11 million.

Area: 447,400 square kilometres.

Capital: Tashkent (population 2.1 million).

President: Islam Karimov.

Neighbouring states: Afghanistan, Kazakhstan, Turkmenistan, Tajikistan and Kyrgyzstan.

GDP:

1990 GDP: 32,430 million roubles.

1990 GDP per capita: 1,579 roubles.

1991 GNP per capita: $1,350.

Exports and Imports:

1990 total exports: 7,702 million roubles, of which:
foreign exports: 813 million roubles,
inter-republic exports: 6,889 million roubles.

1990 total imports: 12,289 million roubles, of which:

foreign imports: 1,296 million roubles,
inter-republic imports: 10,993 million roubles.

64 per cent of all exports were to Europe and 23 per cent to Asia. 70 per cent of all imports were from Europe and 17 per cent from Asia.

Grain Production:

1990: 1.89 million tons.

1991: 1.87 million tons.

Cotton Production:

1991: 4.5 million tons.

1992: 4.1 million tons.

Oil and Gas Production:

1991: gas production: 41 billion cubic metres.
1991: oil production: 2.8 million tons.

Armed Forces:

Army: 15,000 men under joint CIS control.
National Guard of one brigade of 700 men. More to be formed.

Sources: World Bank, IMF, Military Balance, Government of Uzbekistan.

Chronology

500 BC Samarkand founded by Sogdian king Afriasab.

334 BC Alexander the Great conquers Samarkand.

654 AD Arab armies first cross the Amudarya river.

874-999 Samanid empire based in Bukhara rules Uzbek region.

1220 Genghis Khan ravages Bukhara and Samarkand.

1369 Tamerlane makes Samarkand the capital of his empire.

1405 Tamerlane dies.

1417 Registan Madrasah in Samarkand built by Ulug Beg.

1500 Uzbek Shaybani Khan captures Bukhara and sets up Uzbek state.

1826-60 Amir of Bukhara, Nasrullah Khan, consolidates state power.

1861-65 American Civil War increases demand for Central Asian cotton.

1865 Russians capture Tashkent.

1868 Russians capture Samarkand.

1873 Russia forces treaties with Khiva and Bukhara. Abolition of slavery in these states.

1881 Construction of Trans Caspian Railway begins.

1894 Fortress built by Tsar at Tirmiz to guard Afghan border.

1898 Revolt in Andizan against Russian occupation.

1904 Defeat of Russia by Japan.

1916 Famine in Uzbekistan as Tsar issues conscription orders. Jadid revolt against Russian troops crushed.

1917 March: Jadids hold conference of Turkestan's Muslim leaders. October: Tashkent Soviet assumes authority in Central Asia.

1918 March: Treaty between Amir of Bukhara and Tashkent Soviet. Subsequently, Basmachi revolt begins in the Ferghana valley.

1920 September: General Frunze captures Bukhara.

Amir flees to Afghanistan. Khanates of Khiva and Bukhara become People's Republics.

1924 27 October: The Soviet Socialist Republic of Uzbekistan is born. 16,000 cadres are purged from the CPU on Stalin's orders.

1929 Arabic script for Uzbek language replaced by Latin script

1932 March: Karakalpak Autonomous Soviet Socialist Republic is created.

1936 Karakalpak ASSR is transferred from Kazakhstan to Uzbekistan.

1938 President of Uzbekistan, Faizullah Khojaev, and Akmal Ikramov, secretary-general of CPU, are executed after treason trial.

1940 Latin script replaced by Cyrillic script.

1941 22 June: Tamerlane's tomb is exhumed. Hitler invades Russia.

1959 March: Sharif Rashidov becomes first secretary of CPU.

1963 19 September: 40,000 sq. kms. are transferred from Kazakhstan to Uzbekistan by order of the Supreme Soviet.

1966 25 April: Earthquake destroys much of Tashkent.

1983 October: First secretary Sharif Rashidov is removed from office and charged with corruption.

1989 26 May: Birlik party is founded.

3-4 June: Riots in Tashkent and Ferghana between Uzbeks and Meskhetian Turks. One hundred dead.

1990 February: Birlik splits into two. Erk party formed.

24 March: Islam Karimov elected as president.

20 June: Uzbekistan declares its sovereignty.

1991 20 August: Coup attempt in Moscow. Karimov supports coup.

31 August: Uzbekistan declares its independence.

14 September: CPU becomes the People's Democratic Party.

22 November: Birlik registered as a movement but not as a party.

29 December: Karimov wins election for president with 85.9 per cent of the vote. Mohammed Salih of Erk wins 12.4 per cent of the vote.

1992 16 January: Food riots in Tashkent; twenty-one students killed.

February: US Secretary of State James Baker visits Tashkent.

17 March: Crackdown on Islamic fundamentalists in Namangan, seventy people arrested.

April: Tamerlane declared Uzbek national hero and replaces Lenin Status on Tamerlane Boulevard, Tashkent.

May: All Uzbek soldiers of CIS forces recalled home.

30 June: Abdulrahim Pulatov, head of Birlik, beaten up in his office.

12 October: Afghan president Burhanuddin Rabbani meets Karimov in Tashkent. Afghan—Uzbek reconciliation.

8 December: New constitution passed. Elections promised for 1993; and Parliament to be reduced from 500 to 150 members.

9 December: Birlik leaders arrested by Uzbek KGB at Beshkek human rights conference anddriven back to Tashkent jail. Birlik is later banned. Independent newspaper. *The Businessman* is also banned.

December: Uzbek jets and helicopter gunships help Tajik communist forces capture Dushanbe.

19 December: Uzbek helicopter gunship short down by Tajik rebels.

1993 5 January: At Heads of State meeting five Central Asian states decide to create a Union of Central Asian people. They criticize the CIS.

21 January: Supreme Court suspends activities of Birlik for three months.

22 January: At CIS summit, Uzbekistan signs CIS treaty for closer integration.

28 January: Pulatov, leader of Birlik, freed from jail.

16 March: Foreign Minister Sadyk Safaev accuses Pakistan and Afghanistan of helping Tajik fundamentalists. Uzbek troops still deployed in Dushanbe to help Tajik government.

31 March: Malaysian Prime Minister Mahathir Mohammed visits Uzbekistan.

8 April: Turkish president Ozal visits Tashkent; agreements are signed as both leaders oppose Islamic fundamentalism.

10 April: Government arrests Mohammed Salih, chairman of Erk.

22 May: Uzbek newspapers strongly criticize President Nazarbayev.

27 May: Trial of former Vice-President Shukrulla Mirsaidov starts for nepotism and misusing state

resources. He was former Mayor of Tashkent and very popular. Foreign diplomats and journalists removed from the court.

15 June: CIS abandons plans to set up joint armed forces.

22 June: US cuts short visit of Uzbek woman working in the US embassy in Tashkent is beaten up.

23 June: Former Vice President Shukrulla Mirsaidov confirms that he was sentenced to 3 years in jail and then pardoned.

23 July: Saidmukhtar Saidiqasimov made foreign minister. He is a former ambassador to Germany.

9 August: Karimov in Moscow for summit on Tajikistan crisis. He supports Yeltsin in calling for talks between Tajik opposition and government.

2 September: Law passed by parliament to introduce Latin script.

6 September: Russia and five republics including Kazakhstan, Tajikistan and Uzbekistan agree to common rouble zone and the Russian Central Bank as the sole centre for currency distribution.

9 September: Uzbekistan closes borders as cholera spreads in Central Asia. Daewoo setting up US$500 million car plant in Andijan to produce 80,000 cars annually.

16 September: Karimov snubs US Special Envoy Strobe Talbott on human rights and says US should not interfere in Uzbekistan.

18 October: President Rafsanjani of Iran promises in Tashkent to open road and rail links to the sea.

3 November: Uzbekistan criticises Russian rouble zone and threatens to create its own currency. Moscow delays sending new roubles. Uzbekistan and Kazakhstan need to trillion roubles (US$840 million) to maintain solvency.

14 November: New currency, the Sum introduced. Rouble crashes against dollar. Rift with Moscow widens.

17 November: Russian Foreign Minister Andrei Kozyrev in Tashkent as Uzbeks criticise Russia's currency policy.

5 December: Lonrho signs US$250 million deal to develop a gold mine near Zarafshan. Lonrho has five companies in Uzbekistan.

Kazakhstan

Data

Population: 17 million. (Kazakhs 42 per cent, Russian 36 per cent, one hundred other ethnic groups also inhabit the Republic).

Total labour force: 9.2 million.

Area: 2,717,300 square kilometres.

Capital: Alma Ata (population 1.2 million). There are eighty-seven other towns and cities, including Karaganda (614,000). Tselinograd (277,000), Petropavlosk (241,000), Chimkent.

President: Nursultan Nazarbayev.

Neighbouring states: Russia, Turkmenistan, Uzbekistan, Kyrgyzia, China. GDP:

1990 GDP: 45,322 million roubles.

1990 GDP per capita: 2,706 roubles.

1991 GDP: 76,678 million roubles.

1991 industry share of GDP: 30.4 per cent.

1991 agriculture share of GDP: 26.2 per cent.

1991 GNP per capita $2,470.

Exports and Imports:

1990 total exports: 9,488 million roubles, of which: foreign exports: 1,039 million roubles, inter-republic exports: 8,449 million roubles.

1990 total imports: 16,450 million roubles, of which: foreign imports: 1,900 million roubles, inter-republic imports: 14,550 million roubles.

1992 total exports to countries outside the CIS were $1,489 million and total imports were $469 million.

65 per cent of all exports were to Europe and 18 per cent to Asia. 72 per cent of all imports were from Europe and 18 per cent from Asia. Kazakhstan's largest trading partner outside the CIS is China (1992: exports to China were worth $228 million and imports were worth $204 million).

Grain Production:

1990: 28.5 million tons.

1991: 11.9 million tons.

1992: 32 million tons.

Oil Production:

1991: 26 million tons.

1992: 28 million tons.

1992: 8 million tons to Russia.

Estimated oil reserves: 100 billion barrels.

Estimated gas reserves: 2.4 trillion cubic metres.

Minerals:

Kazakhstan has 60 per cent of the mineral resources of the former Soviet Union; it has ninety minerals in all.

1991: Kazakhstan mined 130 million tonnes of coal or a quarter of the former Soviet Union's total. Kazakhstan produced 7 per cent of the former Soviet Union's gold, and 50 per cent of its silver. Kazakhstan also produces lead, copper, zinc, cadmium, iron ore, beryllium, manganese, chrome, nickel, cobalt, bauxite, and industrial diamonds. It has the largest uranium mines in the world.

Armed Forces:

Army: 63,000 men under joint CIS control.

Strategic nuclear force of 104 SS-18 Satan rockets with more than 1,000 warheads, 40 bombers.

National Guard of 5,000 men to be formed.

Sources: IMF, World Bank, Caravan Business News (Alma Ata), Ernst and Young, Military Balance, Government of Kazakhstan

Chronology

600-1200 AD Some Turkic tribes united by legendary figure Alasha Khan in southern Siberia, forerunner of Kazak people.

1200-1500 Kazakh tribes migrate southward from Siberia.

1218 Central Asia devasted by Mongol hordes under Genghis Khan.

1500-1600 Kazakh chiefs resist Uzbek confederacy. Founding of the three Ordas. Kazakhs convert to Islam.

1731-42 Kazakh ordas submit to Russian protection.

1757 Qirot tribes, who devastated Kazakhs, defeated by Chinese.

1783-1970 Kazakhs lose 1 million people in anti-Russian revolts, famine and migration.

1822-48 Kazakh territory incorporated into Russia.

1853 Russians capture Kazakh seat of resistance at Kzyl—Orda.

1854 Vierny, later Alma Ata, is founded by the Russians.

1860 Sino—Russian Treaty, which establishes the formal border with Chinese Xinjiang, further dividing ethnic groups such as the Kyrgyz, Kazakhs and Uighurs.

1864 Russians capture Chimkent.

1891 Some 1 million Russian migrants move into Kazakhstan.

1905 Alash Orda, the Kazakh nationalist party created.

1916 Major anti-Russian revolt by the Kazakh—Kyrgyz tribes. Several hundred thousand migrate to China.

1917 Alash Orda sets up independent government.

1920 Alash Orda joins Bolsheviks.

1920 26 August: The Kazakh Autonomous Soviet Socialist Republic is set up.

1928 First of many purges of Kazakh nationalists from CPKZ.

1930-31 Forced collectivization of Kazakh—Kyrgyz nomads. Tens of thousands killed or migrate.

1936 5 December: The Kazakh Soviet Socialist Republic is founded.

1941 Ethnic groups from Russia sent to Kazakhstan by Stalin.

1954 February: Virgin Lands Scheme begins. One million migrants from other republic arrive.

1964-86 Dinmukhamed Kunayev is first secretary of CPKZ.

1986 17 December: Alma Ata riots begin after Kunayev is removed from office and replaced by a Russian, Gennady Kolbin. Seventeen people are killed and hundreds are injured as riots spread to twelve other towns.

1989 28 February: Nevada—Semipalatinks movement founded.

March: Nursultan Nazarbayev becomes first secretary of the CPKZ.

1990 12 January: Radbek Nisanbai becomes grand mufti of Kazakhstan as new Islamic Religious Board is set up.

February 22: Nazarbayev is re-elected as first secretary and chairman of the Supreme Soviet.

24-26 May: International anti-nuclear conference in

Alma Ata organized by Nevada—Semipalatinsk movement.

26 October: Kazakhstan declares its sovereignty.

1991 20 August: Coup attempt in Moscow.

7 September: CPKZ renamed the Socialist Party.

5 October: Nevada movement turns itself into the People's Congress of Kazakhstan.

1 December: Nazarbayev elected President in the first direct presidential elections, winning 99.8 per cent of the vote.

16 December: Kazakhstan announces its independence.

21 December: CIS formed in Alma Ata.

1992 January-February: Trade, economic agreements signed with China. Opening of railway line between Kazakhstan and China.

26 May: Russia and Kazakhstan sign military and economic agreement.

June: Semipalatinks declared an ecological disaster zone.

29 November: Kazakhstan joins Economic Co-operation Organization (ECO).

20 December: Russia and Kazakhstan endorse call for new, tighter core for Commonwealth.

1993 3 January: START-2 signed in Moscow between Bush and Yeltsin to eliminate three quarters of their 20,000 nuclear warheads by 2003.

5 January: At heads of state meeting five Central Asian states decide to create a Union of Central Asian People.

21 January: Russia demands control of all nuclear weapons from the CIS. Ukraine, Belarus and Kazak nuclear weapons would become part of Russian strategic forces.

28 January: Kazakh Parliament passes new constitution. Kazakh language made the official state language, but Russian decl single military space and single rouble zone.

6 April: After four years of talks, US oil company Chevron signs final agreement with Kazakhstan to develop the Tenghiz oilfield.

16 April: CIS summit in Minsk. Nazarbayev says seven CIS states will form a closer Union by May, including a single rouble zone.

29 April: State Committee on Statistics says economic indicators for the first quarter of 1993 worse than 1992.

13 June: Seven Western oil firms form consortium with Kazakhstan to explore 1000 kms area in Caspian Sea.

15 June: CIS abandons plans to set up joint armed forces.

27 July: IMF approves US$86 credit for Kazakhstan to help transform the economy.

6 August: Nazarbayev in Moscow for summit meeting on Tajikistan calls for greater economic and political union with Russia. Says Islamic fundamentalism a threat to Central Asia and Russia also.

3 September: Chevron agrees with Russia to build 960 km pipeline to carry Tenghiz oil to Black Sea port of Novorossiysk at a cost of US$1.2 billion.

7 September: Russia and five republics including

Kazakhstan, Tajikistan and Uzbekistan agree to common rouble zone and the Russian Central Bank as the sole centre for currency distribution.

13 September: Cholera closes schools in Alma Ata.

18 September: President Mitterand in Alma Ata gives loan of US$50 dollars and 15 contracts worth US$90 million signed with French firms.

29 September: Kazakhstan, Kyrgyzstan, Pakistan and China open talks or Karakorum Highway links to Central Asia.

21 October: Nazarbayev in China to sign friendship treaty but both countries fail to resolve border dispute and deployment of Chinese troops along 1700 km border.

25 October: US Secretary of State Christopher in Alma Ata promises US 85 million for the dismantling of Kazakh nuclear weapons but Nazarbayev refuses to five a timetable. A total US 145 million promised by US to Kazakhstan in economic aid. President Rafsanjani of Iran visits Kazakhstan.

3 November: Kazakhstan criticises Russia for demanding gold reserves in exchange for supplies of roubles.

15 November: Kazakhstan introduces new currency, the Tenge and abandons rouble zone.

25 November: President Nazarbayev blames Russia for ruining rouble zone and says the policy of protecting Russians is like expansionist moves by Hitler.

9 December: Parliament dissolves itself to hold elections on March 7. 350 deputies resign and

local councils also resign. Special powers given to Nazarbayev in interim period.

Kyrgyzstan

Data

Population: 4.4 million, (Kyrgyz 52.4 per cent, Russian 21.5 per cent, Uzbek 12.9 per cent, while eighty other ethnic groups also inhabit the Republic).

Total labour force: 1.75 million.

Area: 198,500 square kilometres.

Capital: Beshkek (population 600,000).

President: Askar Akaev.

Neighbouring countries: China, Uzbekistan, Kazakhstan, Tajikistan.

GDP:

1990 GDP: 8,320 million roubles.

1990 GDP per capita: 1,893 roubles.

1991 GNP per capita: $1,550.

Exports and Imports:

1990 total exports: 2,006 million roubles, of which: foreign exports: 52 million roubles, inter-republic exports: 1,954 million roubles.

1990 total imports: 3,669 million roubles, of which: foreign exports: 759 million roubles, inter-republic exports: 2,910 million roubles.

61 per cent of total exports were to Europe and 35 per cent to Asia. 66 per cent of total imports were from Europe and 17 per cent from Asia.

Wheat Production:

1990: 1.5 million tons.

1991: 1.46 million tons.

1992: 1 million tons.

Armed Forces:

Army: 8,000 men under joint CIS control

National forces to be formed of approximately 5,000 men.

Sources: World Bank, IMF, Military Balance, Government of Kyrgyzstan

Chronology

1500 BC Early Turkic tribes including Kyrgyz inhabit southern Siberia.

800 BC Saka kingdom in present territory of Kyrgyzstan.

500 AD Kazakh—Kyrgyz migrate south from Siberia.

1100 Osh becomes centre of Islamic scholarship.

1207 Genghis Khan defeats his Mongol rival at Tokmak. Kyrgyz later defeated by Genghis Khan.

1500 Babar takes refuge in Kyregyzstan. Kara—Kyrgyz or Black Kyrgyz established as separate group from Kazakhs.

1856 Russians first map out Lake Issyk-Kul.

1959-60 Thousands of Kyrgyz die in freezing winter.

1860 Sino-Russian Treaty which established the border with Xinjiang divides ethnic groups such as the Kyrgyz, Kazakhs and Uighurs.

1860-70 Kyrgyz tribes accept Russian control. Land given to Russian settlers.

1916 Revolt by Kyrgyz and Kazakhs against Russia.

1918 30 April: Kyrgyzstan becomes part of the Turkestan Autonomous Soviet Socialist Republic within the Russian Federation.

1924 Kyrgyz Autonomous Region formed.

1925 Beshkek made the capital and renamed Frunze (1926).

1926 1 February: First purges of Kyrgyz communists from the CPK begin. Kyrgyz Autonomous Soviet Socialist Republic is created.

1936 5 December: Soviet Socialist Republic of Kyrgyzia created.

1961-85 Turdakun Usubaliev first secretary of the CPK.

1978 New constitution adopted.

1985 First Secretary of the CPK Usubaliev retires. Elections to the Supreme Soviet. Absamat Masaliyev is elected as first secretary.

1989 March: Ashar becomes first political opposition group.

1990 10 April: Absamat Masaliyev re-elected as first secretary of CPK.

3 June: Rioting in Osh between Uzbeks and Kyrgyz.

28 October: Askar Akaev elected President of Supreme Soviet.

12 December: Kyrgyzstan announces full sovereignty.

1991 20 August: Coup attempt in Moscow. Akaev supports Yeltsin.

31 August: Kyrgyzstan declares independence.

1993 22 January: AT CIS summit, Kyrgyzstan signs treaty for closer integration.

3 March: A battalion of Kyrgyz peacekeeping troops sent to Afghan—Tajik border.

17 April: During debate on new constitution, Parliament agree on a new 105-member single house to replace Soviet-style system.

24 April: President Akaev visiting Tokyo, says his country may introduce a new currency, the som, soon.

5 May: New constitution adopted by Supreme Soviet.

10 May: Government abandons rouble zone and adopts the Som as the new currency.

14 May: World Bank approves a credit of $60 million for Kyrgyzstan.

22 May: President Akaev in Washington. US approves loan of US$100m, Japan pledges US$60m, Switzerland US$60m.

29 May: Akaev apologises to Karimov for not informing him about currency change.

13 June: 1500 factories lay off workers and production because of Sum. Trading partners unwilling to offer raw materials.

21 June: President Askar Akaev visits Iran and signs 7 agreements. But relations strained after he promises to open Kyrgyz embassy in Jerusalem.

5 July: Russian Defence Minister Pavel Grachev signs agreements on military cooperation with of Kyrgyz Defence Committee, Dzhanibek Umetaliev.

20 July: Monthly inflation rate has dropped since introduction of the Sum. But many factories closed down and foreign suppliers are refusing to accept the new currency.

7 August: Akaev in Moscow for summit on Tajikistan crisis, says Islamic fundamentalism on the decline and conflict caused by clan rivalries. Calls for compromise and talks.

24 August: Stringent budgetary controls declared. No more funds for state-owned industries, redundancies in many ministries and many industries will pay 5 per cent of sales revenue into a social protection fund.

10 December: Vice President Felix Kulov resigns after being accused of involvement in illegal gold trading. PM Tursunbek Chingyshev denies involvement.

Tajikistan

Data

Population: 5.4 million people (Tajiks 58.8 per cent, Uzbeks 23 per cent, Russians 11 per cent. Tartar, German, Ukrainian and Kyrgyz are 1 per cent each of the population).

Total labour force: 1.9 million.

Area: 143,100 square kilometres.

Capital: Dushanbe (population 600,000).

President: Rakhmon Nabiev 23 September 1991 to 7 September 1992. Akbarsho Iskandarov 7 September 1992 to 19 November 1992. Ali Rakhmanov from 19 November..

Neighbouring countries: China, Afghanistan, Uzbekistan, Kyrgyzstan.

GDP:

1990 GDP: 7,112 million roubles.

1990 GDP per capita: 1,341 roubles.

1991 GNP per capita: $1,050.

Exports and Imports:

1990 total exports: 1,999 million roubles, of which:

foreign exports: 356 million roubles.

inter-republic exports: 1,643 million roubles.

1990 total imports: 3,464 million roubles, of which:

foreign exports: 383 million roubles.

inter-republic exports: 3,081 million roubles.

61 per cent of total exports were to Europe and 18 per cent to Asia. 67 per cent of total imports were from Europe and 17 per cent from Asia.

Grain Production:

1990: 3.03 million tons.

1991: 2.83 million tons.

Cotton Production:

1991: 600,000 tons (estimate).

1992: 120,000 tons (estimate).

Aluminium Production:

1990: 520,000 tonnes.

1991: 370,000 tonnes.

1992: 200,000 tonnes.

Oil Production:

1989: 300,000 tonnes.

1990: 90,000 tonnes.

Armed Forces:

Army: 6,000 men under joint CIS command. Bolstered by another 5,000 during civil war in 1992-93.

National forces to be created. Numerous political militias exist.

Sources: World Bank, IMF, Military Balance, Government of Tajikstan.

Chronology

329 BC Alexander invades Tajik region and creates two new cities near present-day Termiz and Khodjent.

300-140 BC Bactrian kingdom in Tajikistan.

400 AD Turkic invasions begin.

654 Arabs first cross the Oxus river.

874-999. Saminid empire. Golden era of Persian culture.

980 Ibn Sina (Avincenna) born near Bukhara. Considered to be Tajik national hero.

1220 Genghis Khan ravages Tajikistan and sacks Termiz.

1273 Marco Polo crosses the Pamirs.

1380 Tamerlane begins campaign to conquer Central Asia.

1762 Manchus annex eastern Turkestan and Tajikistan.

1868 Russia annexes northern Tajikistan.

1884 Anglo—Russian Boundary Commission is set up.

1894 Fortress built at Termiz to guard Afghan border.

1918 February: Kokand captured by Bolsheviks.
April: Basmachi rebellion begins. Civil war begins.

1921 February: Red Army enters Dushanbe.

1922 4 August: Enver Pasha is killed by Red Army.

1923 Famine and epidemics kill thousands.

1924 1924 October: Tajik Autonomous Soviet Socialist Republic (SSR) is created as part of the Uzbek SSR.

1925 January: Gorno-Badakhshan Autonomous Region is created.

1929 15 October: The Tajik Soviet Socialist Republic is created.

1927-31 Several purges of CPTJ.

1931 Jabar Rasulov vecomes first secretary of the CPTJ.

1937 Major purge of CPTJ.

1961 Jabar Rasulov becomes first secretary of the CPTJ.

1979 December: Soviet troops invade Afghanistan.

1982 April: First secretary of CPTJ, Jabar Rasulov, dies.

1982-85 Rakhmon Nabiev is first secretary of CPTJ.

1989 April: Soviet forces complete withdrawal from Afghanistan.

1990 February: Riots in Dushanbe over the resettlement of Armenian refugees. Dozens of people are killed.

1991 August: President Kakhar Makhamov supports Moscow coup.

7 September: President Makhamov is forced to resign. Replaced by Kadriddin Aslonov.

23 September: President Aslonov is replaced by Rakhmon Nabiev.

24 November: General elections. Rakhmon Naviev wins 58 per cent of the vote.

1992 March: beginning of fifty-one days of demonstrations by the opposition.

25 April: Kabul falls to the Afghan Mujheddin.

6 May: Three people killed during demonstrations. Nabiev invokes state of emergency and curfew in Dushanbe.

7 May: Nabiev forms National Reconciliation government with opposition. Demonstrations continue.

12 May: All parties agree to implement agreement.

28 June: 100 people killed in fighting near Kurgan Tube.

31 August: Armed groups take over Parliament building.

7 September: Nabiev is forced to resign. Replaced by Acting President Akbarsho Iskandrov. Kuliab forces attack Kurgan Tube.

27 September: Kuliab forces capture four Russian tanks and seize Kurgan Tube. The next day, Russia orders 2,000 more troops to Tajikistan.

24-25 October: coup attempt in Dushanbe by Kuliab forces.

31 October: UN Security Council appeals for end to fighting.

4 November: Summit meeting in Moscow of all Central Asian leaders to discuss Tajik crisis.

19 November: President Iskandarov resigns at meeting of Parliament in Khodjent. Ali Rakhmanov elected acting President.

22 November: Abdulmalek Abdulajanov becomes Prime Minister. He appeals to Central Asian states to send troops.

23 November: 800 casualties as refugees from Kurgan Tube are attacked near Dushanbe.

25 November: Interior ministry says 50,000 killed in the fighting since June.

5 December: Sixty people killed in Dushanbe as communist militias try to capture Dushanbe but fail.

7 December: 60,000 refugees stranded on Afghan border having fled fighting in Shartuz. Many deaths reported. Russian army calls on Islamic militants to leave Dushanbe.

9 December: 200 refugees die trying to cross Amudarya river to Afghanistan. Other stranded on border. Bread rationing in Dushanbe.

11 December: Dushanbe falls to pro-communist forces. New president and Prime Minister fly in from Khodjent. Islamic forces take up positions outside the city. Fighting begins.

18 December: Islamic rebels regroup around Kofernikhon. Government forces are helped by Uzbek jets and soldiers.

19 December: 150 people are killed in fighting. Uzbek helicopter gunship is shot down by rebels.

22 December: Kofernikhon falls to the government after heavy fighting. Rebels retreat to Pamirs and to Afghan border.

30 December: Government forces capture Pyanj as thousands more refugees flee south to Afghanistan.

1993 7 January: Emergency and curfew declared in Dushanbe.

24 January: President says 3,000 more CIS troops to patrol Afghan border. Four battalions to reinforce the 3,000 troops already on border. State of emergency declared on Afghan border.

19 February: Government launches offensive against rebels stronghold in Romit Gorge, outside Dushanbe.

22 February: Government captures three rebel strongholds, including Garm. CIS forces helping government.

16 March: Government accuses Pakistan and Afghanistan of helping Tajik rebels.

30 March: Popular Front leader Sanjak Safarov is killed.

April: Government kills thirty-two rebels near Kofernikhon.

1 May: UN Secretary-General names Iraqi diplomat Ismat Kattani as his Special UN Envoy for Tajikistan.

9 May: Government accuses rebels of planning invasion from northern Afghanistan. Eighty-six rebels killed on border by CIS forces.

24 May: UNHCR repatriates some 300 refugees to Tajikistan from Afghanistan. More to follow.

31 May: Tajikistan and Russia tell Kabul to enforce order on its border after 3 Russian soldiers killed on Tajik border.

20 June: Garobsho Shahbosov, Chairman of Badakhshan parliament says Badakhsan no longer pursuing independence and it cannot

survive without central government. First food convoys reach Khorog since the winter.

21 June: Supreme Court bans four opposition parties and confiscates their asset. Criminal charges against their leaders.

26 June: In first parliament session since civil war ended, Rakhmonov pledges to build democracy.

2 July: 50 IRP rebels killed by Russian troops after major incursion into Pyandzh region. Tajik complaint to Kabul government.

14 July: 25 Russian troops killed on border and Russia promises to send more troops, armour and planes. Some 200 Tajik villager died in mortar attacks on villages 13 kms inside Tajik border.

17 July: Russian sends more troops to Tajikistan and shells Afghan villages. Russian Defence Minister Pavel Grachev visit Dushanbe.

20 July: Russian Security Minister Viktor Barannikov warns of Afghan war replay as he visits Afghan border. Russian jets bomb rebel forces near Gayzabad.

22 July: Russia says it has the moral right to launch raids into northern Afghanistan.

27 July: Tajik Foreign Minister Rashid Alimov offers 4-way talks with Russian, Uzbekistan and Afghanistan but refuses to talk to the opposition.

28 July: Some 200 Afghan and Tajik rebels killed as they try to cross Tajik border. Week long offensive against rebels around Vari continues.

30 July: Yeltsin orders more troops to Dushanbe and says he will apply to the UN to give them UN status. Grenade explodes outside office of US diplomat in Dushanbe.

1 August: IRP leader Sharif Himmartzade, deported from Pakistan to Kabul, says he is ready for talks with Moscow but not Dushanbe. Offensive starts in Tavildara region of Badakhshan after 4 soldiers are killed. Russian aircraft bomb Afghan villages. Kabul says 300 Afghan villagers killed so far.

6 August: Summit talks start in Moscow between Yeltsin and Central Asian leaders and Tajik President Imamali Rakhmonov.

9 August: Yeltsin urges Tajikistan to start talks with opposition after summit. Also calls for UN observers on Tajik-Afghan border. Tajik FM Rashid Alimov says Tajiks ready for talks.

10 August: Tajik forces recapture Khaburabad pass linking Khorog with Dushanbe after 1-day offensive against rebels. 60 reported killed in fighting.

11 August: Afghan Foreign Minister Amin Arshalla holds successful talks in Dushanbe to control cross border fighting. But I Kazakh and 4 Russian soldiers kidnapped and taken into Afghanistan, in a bid to sour talks.

18 August: Tajik refugees in Afghanistan suffering from cholera and malnutrition. Russia says 14 training camps in northern Afghanistan being run by Afghan Mujheddin for Tajiks.

19 August: UN Special Envoy to Tajikistan Esmat Kittani begins five days trip to Kabul and Tajikistan.

24 August: UN Security Council appeals for end civil war and urges government to open talks with the opposition.

25 August: CIS Defence Ministers set up a coalition

force to control Tajik insurgency under Russian General Boris Pyankov.

26 August: Tajik court gives death sentence to IRP presidium member Ajit Aliyev, after he is found guilty of treason.

28 August: Tajik President visits Kabul for 3 days with 40 strong delegation to discuss border crisis and the release of Russian soldiers. Tajik Airways plane crashes between Khorog-Dushanbe. 65 people killed.

30 August: Tajik President leaves Kabul with kidnapped Russian soldiers.

9 September: Russian Foreign Minister Andrei Kozyrev in Dushanbe urges Tajiks to talk to opposition.

10 September: Tajik rebels attack munitions depots outside Dushanbe and cause massive explosions.

6 October: Russian troops surround 300-400 rebels on border after fierce four day battle. Helicopters and artillery used.

9 October: Tajik rebels capture 3 Russian and 3 Kazakh troops near Khorog but free them later. Fighting between 400 rebels and troops continues for seventh day on border.

25 October: Russian border troops again shell Afghan territory around Imamsahib.

25 November: Russian troops kill 20 Tajik rebels on border.

Turkmenistan

Data

Population: 4.2 million (Turkmen 72 per cent, Uzbeks 13 per cent, Russians 12.6 per cent).

Total labour force: 1.847 million.

Area: 488,000 square kilometres.

Capital: Askhabad 400,000 people. Other cities, Cardzou (162,000 people)

President: Saparmurad Niyazov.

Neighbouring states: Kazakhstan, Uzbekistan, Iran and Afghanistan..

GDP:

1990 GDP: 7,344 million roubles.

1990 GDP per capita: 2,002 roubles.

1991 GNP per capita: $1,700.

Exports and Imports:

1990 total exports: 2,641 million roubles, of which:

foreign exports: 172 million roubles.

inter-republic exports: 2,469 million roubles.

1990 total imports: 3,608 million roubles, of which:

foreign exports: 685 million roubles.

inter-republic exports: 2,923 million roubles.

63 per cent of total exports were to Europe and 22 per cent to Asia. 71 per cent of total imports were from Europe and 20 per cent from Asia.

Oil and Gas Production:

1989: 5.4 million tons of oil, 85 billion cubic metres of gas.

1991: 5.4 million tons of oil, 80.4 billion cubic metres of gas.

1992: 5.2 million tons of oil, 55 billion cubic metres of gas.

8.1 trillion cubic metres of proven gas reserves.

700 million tonnes of proven petroleum reserves.

Cotton Production:

1991: 1.4 million tonnes.

Grain Production:

1990: 4.44 million tonnes.

1991: 4.47 million tonnes.

Armed Forces:

Army: 34,000 men under joint CIS command.

National forces to be formed.

Sources: World Bank, IMF, Military Balance, Government of Turkmenistan.

Chronology

329-327 BC Alexander the Great conquers the region.

200 BC-AD 10 Parthian civilization.

1000-1100 AD Turkmen migrate to Caspian region from the east.

1741 Turkmen first resist and then join armies of Persian king Nadir Shah.

1813 Russia defeats Persia and enters Turkman area.

1834 Russia starts building forts in Turkman territory.

1870 Turkmen being guerrilla war against Russians.

1873 Khiva is captured by Russians.

1881 Russians capture fort of Geok Tepe and massacre 6,000 Turkmen.

1886 Turkmen territory is annexed by Russia.

1900-1905 Strikes in Ashkhabad by Russian workers.

1916 Junaid Khan captures Khiva.

1919 Bolsheviks capture Khiva.

1919-27 Guerrilla war against Russians led by Junaid Khan.

1918 Turkmenistan becomes part of Turkestan Autonomous Republic.

1915 14 February: Soviet Socialist Republic of Turkmenistan is created.

1928 Collectivization begins.

1930 Purges against CPT members begin.

1948 6 October: Earthquake destroys Ashkhabad.

1969-86 Mukhamednazar Gapurov is first secretary of CPT.

1987 November: First protest demonstrations in Askhabad by Afghan war veterans.

1988 May: Demonstrations in Ashkhabad over unemployment.

1989 Six hundred academics and intellectuals form the first 'informal' group, named Agzbirlik.

1990 August 22: Sovereignty of Turkmenistan is declared.

26 October: 98 per cent of the population vote for President Saparmuradov Niyazov in first presidential elections.

1991 August: Coup attempt in Moscow is supported by Niyazov.

1992 March: New constitution is adopted.

22 June: Niyazov is re-elected President winning 99.5 per cent of the vote.

1993 22 January: Turkmenistan refuses to sign CIS treaty for closer integration.

18 March: President Niyazov vows to stop Islamic fundamentalism and refuses to allow political parties.

21 April: Turkish businessmen plan to invest $800 million in Turkmenistan.

14 May: AT CIS summit in Moscow, Turkmenistan refuses to support economic union for CIS members.

25 October: President Rafsanjani of Iran signs deals in Turkmenistan on transport and to build a pipeline for export of Turkmen gas to the West via Iran; 160 km. Railway link between Iran and Turkmenistan being completed.

29 October: New currency Manat replaces rouble. US $300 million of reserves set aside to back it. Huge price rises as subsidies lifted.

Bibliography

Books

1. A.M. Adshead, *Central Asia in World History*. Published by Maciwllan, London, 1993.
2. Alexandre A. Bennigson and S. Enders Wimbush, *Muslim National Communism in the Soviet Union*, Published by the University of Chicago Press, USA, 1990.
3. A. Solzhenitsyn, *Rebuilding Russia*, London, 1992.
4. Alexandre A. Bennigson and S Endrs Wimbush, *Muslim of the Soviet Empire, A Guide*, C. Hurst, London, 1985.
5. Ahmad Rashid, *The Resurgence of Central Asia,* London, 1994.
6. Dodar and Branson, *Gorbachev Heretic Icon in the Kremlin,* London, 1990.
7. Geoffrey Wheeler, *The Modern History of Soviet Central Asia*. Weiden Field and Nicolson, London, 1964.
8. Gragam H Fuller, *Central Asia, The New Geo-Politics,* Santa Monica, California, 1992.
9. Hamid Algar, *Islam and Revolution; Writings and Declarations of Imam Khumeini*, Berkeley, 1981.

10. J. Crichlow, *Nationalism in Uzbekistan: A Soviet Road to Sovereignty*, Westview, USA, 1991.

11. Milan Hauner, *What is Asia for us,* Unwin Hyman, London, 1990.

12. Michael Kaser and Santosh Mehrotra, *The Central Asian Economics after Independence,* Royal Institute of International Affairs, London, 1992.

13. Martha B. Olcott, *The Kazaskhs,* Hoover Institute at Stanford, California, USA, 1987.

14. Paul Gobl, *Enthnicity and National Conflicts*, Ed. S. Neil MacFarlance, Centre for International Relations, Queens University Canada, 1992.

15. Robert A. Lewis, *Geographic Perspectives on Central Asia*, Routledge, London, 1992.

16. R. Grousset, *The Emire of the Steppes: A History of Central Asia* North Ireland, Rutgers University Press, 1970.

17. Rubin Manatsakanian, *Environmental Legacy of the Former Soviet Republics*. Edinburgh University, 1992.

18. R. Abazov, A Vasilivetski and V. Panomarev, *Islam and Political Struggle in the CIS Countries*, Moscow, 1992.

19. S. Crawshaw, *Goodbye to the USSR: The Collapse of Soviet Power*, London, 1992

20. Vaidyanath, R. *The Foundations of the Soviet Central Asian Republics,* New Delhi, 1990.

Journals

1. A.A. Rizvi. ' ECO for Regional Cohesion', *Pakistan and Gulf Economist,* 1991.

2. Ahmad Rashid, 'Central Asian Republics Must Be Consulted', *Nation,* Lahore, 1991.

3. Ahmad Rashid, 'Muslims Chance to Seek More Power', *Independent,* London, 1991.

4. Ahmad Rashid, ' The Next Frontier', *Far Eastern Economic Review*, 1993.

5. Allen Hatmanek, 'Islamic Revolution and. Jihad Come to the the Former Soviet Central Asia: The Case of Tajikistan', *Central Asian Survey*, Vol. 12, No. 3, 1993.

6. Anthony Benins, 'Aimed to Destabilise Soviets', *Independent*, 1990.

7. Akimove A. V. 'Russia and Central Asia: Perspectives of Economic Integration', *Orient*, No. 4, 1994.

8. *Asia,* Moscow, No. 1, 1994.

9. Bess Brown, 'The Islamic Renaissance Party in Central Asia', REF/RL Research Report, 1991.

10. Bess Brown, 'The IRP in Central Asia', Research Paper.

11. *Current Digest of the Post-Soviet Press* (CDPSP), vol. XLIV (42), London, 1992.

12. Constantine Michalopoulos and David Tarr, 'Energizing Trade of the States of the Former USSR', *Finance and Development*, 1993.

13. *Central Asian Significant*, 1991.

14. *Financial Times*, 1987.

15. H. Smith, ' The New Russians', *Vintage*, USA, 1990.

16. *Second Revolution*, Indian Centre for Regional Affairs, New Delhi, 1989. Interview with Nursultan Nazarbayev (The Kazak President) in *Moskouskye Novosti*, No. 15, Moscow, 1993.

17. Interview with Islam Karimov (The Uzbek President) *Trade,*_ Moscow, 1993.

18. IMF *Reports* on countries of Central Asia, 1992.

19. Ignor Rotar ' The Bomb placed by the Kremlin Cartographers', *Nezanisimava Gazeta,* Moscow, 1993.

20. *International Life,* Moscow, No. 3, 1993.

Independence, London, 1991.

21. James Critchlow, 'Uzbeks look Askance of Gorbachev's Union Ideas', *RFE/RL Research Report*, 1991.

22. Jeffery Smith, ' Ukraine Ready to Place Warheads Under Supervision', *Dawn,* 1993.

23. Kiaras Gharabaghi, 'Development Strategies for Central Asia in the 1990's in Search of Alternatives', *Third World Quarterly*, Vol. 15, No. 1, London, 1994.

24. *Kessings Record of World Events, New Digest for December 1991*, London, 1991.

25. *Kayhan*, Tehran, 1992.

26. Kesar and Mehrotra, ' Central Asian Economics and Economic Effects of Soviet Dissolution;, Royal Institute of International Affairs, London, 1993.

27. K.N. Pandita, ' The Travails of Tajikistan, *The Pioneer,* New Delhi, 1995.

28. *Kazakhstanskaya Pravda,* Almaty, December, 1995.

29. *Middle East – Contemporary Survey*, London, 1992.

30. Martha Olcott ' Central Asia's Port Empire Politics', *Orbis* , 1995.

31. *Mezhdunarodnaya Zhizn*, Moscow, No. 10, 1995.

32. *National Doctrine of Russia: Problems and Priorities,* Moscow, 1994.

33. *Newsweek,* 1992.

34. Oumirserik Kasenov, ' Central Asia: National, Regional and Global Aspects of Security" in *Himalayan and Central Asian Studies*, Vol. I, No. 1, April - June 1997.

35. *Panorama,* Moscow, No. 45, December 1994.

36. P. Stobdan, 'Central Asian Regional Security', *Strategic Analysis, Vol XV, No. 5*, New Delhi, 1992.

37. Patrick Cockburn, 'Dateline USSR: Ethnic Tremors', *Foreign Policy,* 1989.

38. *Pravda Vostoka*, Moscow, Feb 24., 1995.

39. Ronals Dannreuther, 'Creating New States in Central Asia', *Adelphi Paper,* The International Institutional Legacy of the Former Soviet Republic', Edin. 1992.

40. Reuters, 'Kazaks to Keep Nuclear Arms', *Dawn*, 1992.

41. Rovert V. Barylski, ' Kazakhstan Military Dimension of the State Formation over Centra Asia's Civilizational Fault Lines. Oxford Westview press.

42. Richard F. Staar, *The New Military in Russian.*, Annapolis, Maryland, USA, Naval Institute Press, 1996.

43. Shireen T. Hunter, ' Nationalist Movements in Central Asia' *Current History, Vol 85*, No. 549, 1990.

44. Sanobar Shermatona, ' Who is Fighting Whom in Tajikistan', in *Russia and the Muslim World* No. 46, Moscow, 1996.

45. *Strategic Balance,* 1992.

46. Steve Cole ' The Distant Dream on Russia's Rim' *Dawn* , 1993.

47. *Trud,* January, 1992.

48. US Information Service, 1993.

Index